"Do you want to know what moves God's heart? Caring for those who cannot care for themselves. The Johnson family found this out when they gave their hearts fully to the Lord and fully to the care of young Connor. What was once considered a disability in Connor's life is now his greatest asset—an asset Jesus is using to bless many other families around the globe. *Champion* is a wonderful book of hope and triumph. Read it and let God change your heart."

—*Christine Caine*, bestselling author, founder of A21 and Propel

"I have watched Craig and Samantha Johnson navigate the new season of parenting a child with autism for the last fourteen years. And they have done so with wisdom, courage, and hope. I believe as you read their story you will be inspired and you, too, will find wisdom, courage, and hope."

—*Paul Osteen*, MD

"As a pastor at Lakewood, I have watched closely how the Johnson family responded to the news about their son Connor. They chose, in the middle of great difficulty, to trust God and His Word above what they saw with their eyes and what they heard with their ears. They believed God had a greater purpose for Connor, and they were right. The story you will read in *Champion* is nothing short of amazing. The Johnsons have walked the walk, day in and day out. God has now shared Connor's story around the world, blessing families everywhere. Jesus loves to use 'the least of these' to confound the wise. *Champion* is a book that will open your heart to the beautiful truth that there are no accidental lives—and every life can produce miracles."

—*Pastor John Gray III*, associate pastor, Lakewood Church; author of *I Am Number 8*

"Our family holds Craig Johnson and his family in such high esteem as they have encouraged and championed us personally through the journey of autism. This book is *so* important and timely as we *must* learn to see differently, learn differently, and find a way for *all* people to truly belong and thrive. We have incorporated Champions Club into the soul of our church so that with all our hearts we can honestly say, 'there's a place for you here.'"

—*Darlene Zschech*, Hope Unlimited Church

"I love this family and I love this story. *Champion* is a wonderful example of what it means to trust God by praying bold prayers. After a season of discouragement, knowing their young son would live with autism, the Johnsons decided it was time to get up, believe God, and pray like they had never prayed before. They began with Scriptures and leaned on God's Word every day. Read *Champion*, and you will have a front-row seat to how bold prayers honor God and make a big difference."

—*Mark Batterson*, *New York Times* bestselling author of *The Circle Maker*; lead pastor of National Community Church

"It is my pleasure to give the highest recommendation for Craig Johnson's book *Champion*. As pastors, Craig and I have a lot in common. As fathers, though, we have much more in common: being parents to children who are indeed champions. When my daughter Georgia received a difficult diagnosis, my family was hurt and confused. But as we looked to God, we decided we were going to see this new reality as a blessing. God would turn this into a message of hope. And since then we have not been defined by a diagnosis. Instead, Georgia's testimony is inspiring lives everywhere. The Johnsons believed God was in their diagnosis and through their great faith, God has turned Connor's story into a worldwide movement for good. So many families are now blessed because of Connor and because one family refused to accept a bad diagnosis. Believe what God has to say about your life. Believe that you, too, can be a champion for the Lord."

—*Chad Veach*, lead pastor, Zoe Church; author of *Unreasonable Hope* and *Faith Forward Future*

"In this beautifully written story of tragedy and triumph, Craig Johnson challenges us to a higher level of trust. How do brokenhearted parents move from 'God, why did You let this happen?' to 'Why not trust that God has a bigger plan?' I've watched Craig, Samantha, and Connor live this out. In *Champion*, Craig invites us to experience a miracle, no matter what life throws at us. This is a book that you won't want to put down, a book that could change your next 'Why, God?' moment. Why not believe God for a miracle?"

—*Greg Surratt*, founding pastor, Seacoast Church

"*Champion* is the story of how God uses any and everybody to make a difference—even a child with autism named Connor. Craig Johnson speaks from the heart to show how someone many might consider to be 'the least of these' can cause a ripple with an impact that spans the entire globe and changes countless lives. However, it would be a disservice to think that this book only speaks to the special-needs community. This is a testament to how every life has value and sometimes our purpose is revealed to us in what seems like our darkest moment. The Champions Club is a critical movement that is rapidly expanding to give hope and dignity to millions of people."

—*Chris Dowling*, writer/director of *Where Hope Grows*; producer of *Aspergers Are Us*

"'Even on your worst day, you may become someone else's best hope.' Craig and his beautiful family embody this quote over and over again. Their faith in times of trial and their willingness to help those in need is beyond inspiring. *Champion* shows that every mess can turn into a message and God always has a higher purpose for the pain; we just have to trust and use the tools He's given us. And with *hope*, *love*, and *faith* miracles *do* happen. The Johnson family are the true champions!"

—*Victoria Arlen*, ESPN on-air personality, speaker, actress, model, paralympian Gold Medalist

"Every obstacle is an opportunity to overcome. This is the core message of Pastor Craig Johnson's new book *Champion*. This beautiful, encouraging masterpiece was created to help all people win, especially those who feel the odds are against them. Craig's relentless vulnerability and unmasked transparency will be sure to help you and everyone attached to you. Even if the rest of the people in your world don't read this book (which I pray they do) they'll surely be impacted by it because of the effect it'll have on you. I champion this book because this book has championed me. Thank you, Craig."

—*Chris Durso*, author of *The Heist:*
How Grace Robs Us of Our Shame

"In your hands is a testimony about how the world is being blessed by one young man and God's unfailing love. For the past seven years, I have had the privilege of seeing Pastor Craig and Samantha, Cory, Courtney, and Connor embrace God's plan for their lives and use what is commonly thought of as an insurmountable hurdle, a diagnosis of autism, to further the kingdom of God. Their message is simple: God is faithful, and there is hope and joy in the journey. In my thirty-four years of ministering to Champions and their families in public education and church communities, Pastor Craig Johnson stands alone as the single most driving force in ensuring that these individuals have the resources they need to be prepared and positioned to make a difference in this world."

—*Sandra L. Robinson*, PhD, regional
director of Champions Club

"Pastor Craig Johnson is by far the most humble, godly man I have met, and his story has impacted me immensely. I have been challenged to live beyond my circumstances, dream for the impossible, and allow our awesome God to do what only He can do. *Champion* is a book that captures more than a story and speaks the heart of God. As you read it your faith will be stirred."

—*Andy Kirk*, National Director for Children's
Ministry, Australian Christian Churches

"Craig is one of the most encouraging people I've ever met. His huge heart is a vessel God uses to deliver hope to others, no matter what they may be facing. In this precious book Craig shares his family's story and exhorts us to look at what's going right in life, not what may be going wrong. Connor's life and the Champions Club ministry is changing thousands of families, churches, and communities all over the world. This is an important book for church leaders, friends, and families of children with additional needs and any person who needs an injection of hope and faith—everyone of us! *Champion* will challenge your mind-set, and you will see that 'the least of these' are 'the best of these'!"

—*Nathan McLean*, children's pastor, Hillsong Church Australia

"Craig Johnson is the epitome of a trailblazer. What he, Sam, and the Johnson family have walked through together and *modeled* has inspired so many, including myself, to fight for others in the midst of my own setbacks and challenges. I believe Connor's story and the heart of this book will inspire you to be the champion God's designed you to be!"

—*Nick Nilson*, young adults pastor, Lakewood Church

"Knowing Samantha and Craig for more than a decade, we have seen them raise an amazing family, lead a thriving ministry, and face the challenges of life with a son diagnosed with autism. Everyone should read *Champion* to experience their story and hear how God is using Connor to ignite hope within the most hopeless situations around the world!"

—*Clayton and Ashlee Hurst*, authors of *Hope for Your Marriage*

"In *Champion*, you get invited into Pastor Craig and Samantha's world where you will laugh, cry, and be uplifted as they learn to navigate through the world of autism. Through God's Word they have learned to celebrate the small victories. They know and trust that God has amazing plans for Connor's future."

—*Norma Puga*, regional director of Champions Club

"As a parent of a young adult with exceptional and often critical needs, Pastor Craig's book *Champion* spoke straight to my heart and blessed me to know that there are other parents and families out there struggling with the same issues we have struggled with. It was also a gift to see how God is using the Johnson family for great good, even in the midst of sometimes difficult circumstances."

—*Mary Tutterow*, author of *The Heart of the Caregiver*

"*Champion* challenges the status quo of any diagnosis. God uses all to His glory, and you'll see how He has used one little boy's life to change the world! Read the book and join the movement!"

—*Lisa Birge-Price*, director of Special Needs
Ministries, Champions Club Fresh Start Church,
Egg Harbor Township, New Jersey

"Craig's story proves the power of unswerving hope in God in the midst of difficult circumstances. This book will challenge and inspire you to hold onto hope so that you can be the champion others may need. Jen and I are immensely grateful for Craig's courage to step out and share the vision of Champions Club. Our family and church are eternally different because of his love and God-given vision."

—*Jeremy and Jen DeWeerdt*, senior pastors, City First Church

"Craig Johnson ignites the heart to believe and trust God in spite of any adversity! *Champion* is a must-read for every mom and dad who is believing God for a miracle in their home!"

—*Rev. Adam Durso*, executive director, LEAD.NYC;
NYC Mayor's Clergy Advisory Council

Champion

Champion

HOW ONE BOY'S MIRACULOUS JOURNEY THROUGH AUTISM IS CHANGING THE WORLD

CRAIG JOHNSON

EMANATE
BOOKS

While the Johnson's family story was previously available as the self-published book *Unrehearsed Destiny*, much of the content has been revised and updated from the original manuscript, including new stories and reflections.

Published in Nashville, Tennessee, by Emanate Books, an imprint of Thomas Nelson. Emanate Books and Thomas Nelson are registered trademarks of HarperCollins Christian Publishing, Inc.

Thomas Nelson titles may be purchased in bulk for educational, business, fund-raising, or sales promotional use. For information, please e-mail SpecialMarkets@ThomasNelson.com.

Unless otherwise noted, Scripture quotations are from the Holy Bible, New Living Translation. © 1996, 2004, 2007, 2013, 2015 by Tyndale House Foundation. Used by permission of Tyndale House Publishers, Inc., Carol Stream, Illinois 60188. All rights reserved.

Scripture quotations marked NIV are from the Holy Bible, New International Version®, NIV®. Copyright © 1973, 1978, 1984, 2011 by Biblica, Inc.® Used by permission of Zondervan. All rights reserved worldwide. www.Zondervan.com. The "NIV" and "New International Version" are trademarks registered in the United States Patent and Trademark Office by Biblica, Inc.®

Scripture quotations marked NCV are from the New Century Version®. © 2005 by Thomas Nelson. Used by permission. All rights reserved.

Scripture quotations marked ESV are from the ESV® Bible (The Holy Bible, English Standard Version®). Copyright © 2001 by Crossway, a publishing ministry of Good News Publishers. Used by permission. All rights reserved.

Scripture quotations marked NASB are taken from New American Standard Bible®. Copyright © 1960, 1962, 1963, 1968, 1971, 1972, 1973, 1975, 1977, 1995 by The Lockman Foundation. Used by permission. (www.Lockman.org)

ISBN 978-0-7852-1840-1 (TP)

ISBN 978-0-7852-1841-8 (eBook)

Library of Congress Control Number: 2017956696

Printed in the United States of America

18 19 20 21 22 LSC 10 9 8 7 6 5 4 3 2 1

To my wife, Samantha, and my children, Cory and Courtney. From the very beginning of finding out about Connor's diagnosis you have given yourselves unconditionally to love, care, and believe in him. You are my heroes. Connor, you have changed us so profoundly. I can't put into words what a gift you have been to us. I am a better husband, father, and person because of you, son. I have never loved so deeply until I walked on this journey with you. You're my best friend. I can't wait to see all the incredible ways God will use you in the future.

Contents

Foreword by Joel Osteen

All of us like certainty and the ability to predict what's coming next. But, as we frequently find out, life's not always predictable and can oftentimes take an unexpected turn that seems less than ideal. When this happens, it is easy to lose hope, to focus on what went wrong, and to feel that the wonderful future we designed for ourselves is lost. But it doesn't have to be that way. If we remain in faith, knowing that God is in control, we can embrace a new plan—His plan—one that will not only help us to overcome a painful experience, but one that will lead us to a different and greater purpose.

This is what happened to my friends Craig and Samantha Johnson. They had two beautiful children with a third on the way. When their youngest son Connor was born, he seemed just like their other children, and, as parents do, they began making plans for him. But, at two years of age, they noticed that something didn't seem normal. He wasn't developing and talking like the other children. Soon, Connor was diagnosed with autism.

Given the circumstances, they were discouraged. But as faithful believers, Craig and Samantha understood a simple principle: Don't put a question mark where God put a period. They didn't sit around blaming God or asking why He did this to them, but instead, they embraced the unexpected and began to look for the greater purpose God had for them.

Shortly after the diagnosis, Craig and Samantha began to pray that God would show them how to respond to Conner's needs, and they came to realize that many other families were dealing with similar situations. It was then that God birthed a new dream in their hearts. I remember the day Craig came to me and said that there should be a place for special-needs children at our church; a place where parents could entrust their special-needs children to trained individuals so that they could worship in peace knowing that their children were being cared for.

I loved the idea and soon Craig developed a program and curriculum for special-needs children. We recognized that God was birthing something new in Craig and Samantha, something that would affect the lives of countless other families. So, Lakewood Church started the Champions Club—the first of its kind in the world—and within six months more than three hundred new families with special-needs children joined the church. When I spoke to these families and listened to their stories, it became apparent that God had set in place a higher purpose for Craig, Samantha, and for Conner; and that it would not only affect their lives but would eventually affect thousands of lives across America and around the world.

It wasn't long before other churches, schools, and organizations heard about the Champions Club and began to ask for help to start their own. Craig assembled a team and began helping others around the world launch their own special-needs programs. Now there are more than thirty Champions Clubs in seven different nations, with plans to start hundreds more. This is just the beginning.

I can think of no one better to write this book than Craig Johnson. He and Samantha know what it means to have every plan you've ever made change in a moment. When you encounter that one diagnosis, one unforeseen event, or one instance where you realize that your future looks nothing like you thought it would, don't get discouraged, but instead, turn to God and allow Him to create a new reality, a new destiny, a new purpose. Like Craig, God is counting on you to help others who are facing the same thing you're going through. Out of that pain you're going to discover your new destiny.

This beautiful book will take you on a faith-filled journey that will move you from survivor to victor. In it, Craig will show you how your test can become the very thing that propels you forward and how champions are borne from adversity. I believe after reading these chapters you're going to come out stronger with a new vision for your life and with a new purpose.

Remember, nothing is a surprise to God. He's already designed your life and laid out every piece down to the smallest detail. You may not have foreseen the troubles or rehearsed the life you see in front of you, but, as Craig shares in this book, when it all comes together, every piece is going to fit perfectly in place and that which you thought would harm you will ultimately take you to greater heights. Get ready, you're about to be released into your new destiny—the destiny of a champion!

ONE

The Calm Before the Storm

The best way I can describe it is like a sudden car wreck. Shock. One minute your child behaves one way, and the next minute he doesn't seem like the same child you knew in the first two years of his life. He's stopped talking. He stares off into space with no emotion.

What happened? Did we do something wrong? Is God mad at us? Is this a curse upon our family?

When this happened to us, I even tried to remember the worst sins I had committed between the years 1995 and 2001, thinking if I had only done things differently, maybe this wouldn't have happened. *This burden is so heavy. I'm not sure if I'm strong enough to carry it*, I thought. Then came the ultimate question, the granddaddy of them all, the big one every person asks when they face something that is beyond what their finite human mind can comprehend. If you've been through a tragic situation, failed, lost a loved one, or just received devastating news, then you've asked this question.

Maybe you asked it as tears were pouring down your

1

face. It might have been after you had come to the end of yourself, and you didn't just ask it, you screamed it—at the top of your lungs because you wanted to make sure God heard it. Unfortunately, unbeknownst to you, half the neighborhood heard it. Right before the question you might have even let a word slip out that you shouldn't have. Okay, maybe two words. But you didn't care. The pain was too great to feel embarrassed. You had to ask the only question that came to your mind when you just didn't understand.

Why?

Have you ever asked God why? I'll never forget where I was and what I was feeling when I asked it. But before we go there, let's go back to where the story begins. It's always good to remember where you started so one day you can appreciate how you finished.

The greatest journeys are often the most difficult. In every fairy tale there is usually tragedy and triumph. You can't get to the "happily ever after" unless you're willing to fight for the here and now, and we were about to have the fight of our lives.

We were about to discover that we couldn't plan our lives. We could only allow God to help us navigate through them. Of course, we all think we can plan—or at least manage our time. Our strategy works well until a sudden change in our lives' weather patterns causes the barometer to spin out of control. Chaos blows in like a drizzle, and suddenly it pours down like a flood.

My wife Samantha (Sam) and I had it all planned out. We were going to have our kids early so we could travel the world, footloose and kid-free, at fifty. Goodbye, Lunchables and Happy Meals. Hello, steak and lobster.

I had a vision of driving cross-country in a Winnebago and visiting every major-league baseball park in the United States. I hoped that, by that time, our kids would have graduated from college and landed amazing jobs working for Disney or Apple. We had their lives planned out. Hey, they might even support us in our early retirement. We figured, we gave them life, so the least they could do is give us the retirement we always dreamed of, right?

Sam and I had two children. Cory was born in 1919—I mean 1991. We call him our old man because now, at twenty-seven, he drives so slowly that cement trucks race past him on the freeway. Cory was an old soul and as straight as an arrow even at seven years old. He would say whatever was on his mind, and he would say it like a crotchety old man. Once when Cory was a young boy and we were in a restaurant, someone started smoking next to us. We could see Cory was getting perturbed, and suddenly he yelled out, "Good God, is he smoking a cigarette? He's going to die!" The poor man hid his cigarette and, with his head down, slipped outside, having just been condemned to die by a seven-year-old.

Our daughter, Courtney, arrived in 1993. A born performer, she nearly came out singing "There's No Business Like Show Business" from the Broadway musical *Annie Get Your Gun*. We had our boy and girl, and not only did they keep us entertained, but they were the best two kids any parents could ask for. Considering how many headaches I gave my parents,

I wasn't sure they were mine. My wife assured me they were, so I nodded and went with it.

With an eleven-year-old son, a nine-year-old daughter, and our lives moving along just as we had planned, my wife and I decided, after much prayer and trepidation on my part, that I would get the outpatient surgery that guys get when they are satisfied with the number of children God has given them. For the first time in almost twelve years, we started shopping for a car that wasn't a minivan.

You might think we didn't enjoy being parents, but we loved it. We just figured that, after twenty-two years of commitment to raising our children, there must be some prize at the end of the parenting rainbow. A prize was coming all right, but not the one we expected. I had the dreaded procedure on Thursday, and on Saturday of the same week, my wife Sam walked into our bedroom with a look on her face I had only seen one other time—when our daughter was two years old and decided to draw flowers on the side of our new car with a quarter because she wanted to make a pretty picture to show Daddy when he came home. It was that anxious, *how-am-I-going-to-tell-Craig-what-happened* face.

I looked at her and said, "What's up?" I thought to myself, *Don't tell me Courtney drew daisies on the car again. She's nine years old.*

As I waited for a response, Sam's face started to twist and her eyes squinted as if she had just bitten into a giant lemon.

"I don't know how to tell you this . . . but I'm pregnant," she said.

Now I was the one with the anxious look on my face. The first thing that came out of my mouth was, "How did that happen?"

"What do you mean how did it happen?" she asked. "You know how it happens."

I was so dumbfounded, I felt like I needed "the talk" my dad gave me years ago as an adolescent.

"But I just got all of that taken care of," I said. "How in the world could this have happened?"

You must understand the state of shock we were both in. Of course, my wife was the sane one at the moment. I was the one with a vision of our Winnebago dream driving off the cliff.

"Are you sure?" I asked.

By then she couldn't even speak. All she could do was nod her head as tears of disbelief rolled down her beautiful red cheeks. By then I had come to my senses and I pulled her to me and we hugged and cried—me bellowing louder than her—for the next few minutes.

"Are you okay?" I asked.

"I'm not sure," she said tearfully. "Our life is about to change." Then I went into Batman mode.

"It's okay, honey. We'll figure it out."

She looked up again and said, "Are you okay?"

"I just have one question. Couldn't we have found this out three days earlier, before I went through the gauntlet?"

We started laughing. It was one of the most unexpected and one of the best moments of our lives.

When you experience a big change moment in your life, your dreams have not been lost, but a new destiny is waiting to be found. It will include priceless experiences that will profoundly shape how you view life and what you believe to be important. The ride may get bumpy. Yet, for every pothole in the road, if you will let Him, God will give you a new revelation of grace to fill it. A journey like this will not be what you expected because your life has just moved from the plans of man to the supernatural blueprint of divine providence. Of course, it's hard to tell something that huge has happened, because in the moment, you're just trying to keep your wheels on the road.

Our family was thrilled we were going to have a new addition, and we soon found out it was going to be a boy. Cory was excited that his new brother and *Finding Nemo* were possibly coming out on the same weekend. Courtney was mad it was going to be a boy and not a girl. She wanted someone she could dress up and have tea parties with. I assured her she could still dress up her little brother and have tea parties, to which she replied, grinning, "Yes!"

At 11:00 p.m. on July 6, 2003, Samantha informed me it was time.

"Now?" I asked.

"Yes, now get me to the hospital!"

We piled the family in the minivan in the middle of the

night and sped off. My wife and kids looked stressed, so I thought I would lighten the mood by saying, "Is anyone hungry? I could go for a hamburger."

The kids started yelling, "Dad, we don't have time to eat!" For some reason, my wife wasn't laughing either.

"But I'm hungry," I responded. "Who wants a cheeseburger?"

As I started to jokingly pull into McDonald's, my wife calmly but firmly said, "Unless you want the drive-thru attendant to deliver our son, you had better get me to the place where they have doctors!"

As we drove into the hospital parking lot, I could tell she was getting close. Now I was the one getting stressed. It was after hours, and the main entrance door was locked. So we took off walking around the hospital—my wife having contractions—until we found the emergency room entrance. Sam quietly whispered in my ear, "I'll get you for this."

They rushed my wife to the delivery room as I dropped our kids off in the waiting area. My son said, "Hey, look, *General Hospital* is on TV."

The very next thing we heard was, "Congratulations! It's a boy!"

My wife is fast.

Connor Landon Johnson was born on July 7, 2003, at around 1:00 a.m. He weighed seven pounds, three ounces, but the weight of his life would be much greater than that.

Connor was just like most newborns. He slept a lot and then disbursed strange odors from his diaper, odors that scientists still cannot identify. He was the apple of our eye. The kids loved to hold him. We had season passes to Disneyland, so on the sixth day of his life we took him for a stroller ride through the Magic Kingdom to meet the world. It wiped the poor little guy out. So on the seventh day he rested.

When Connor turned one, we threw a big birthday party that only we would remember. Isn't it funny how a party for a one-year-old is more for the parents than for the kids? But we loved our parent party, and Connor went along with it. When he turned two, he was like any other typical kid. He would play with friends, say "I love you," give us hugs, and eat with both hands. He was the all-American boy. Then, everything changed.

At about two years old, our son was just like our other kids—playful and affectionate. He was fluent in speech, even at such a young age. He loved to talk, but most of all he loved to eat. I knew this child was mine just based on his eating skills. (I'm a foodie, and even to this day my son gets more excited about eating certain foods than any child I've ever known. When you get him something to eat that he likes, his eyes light up like a Christmas tree and a big smile appears on his face.)

Then he started having earaches, and they progressively got worse. We took him to the doctor who said he needed to have tubes put in his ears—not uncommon for young children. The surgery went as expected. Also during this time, our doctor's office wanted to make sure Connor got all his shots.

Although we knew this was a recommended procedure,

we had some concerns—especially so soon after his surgery. But we figured the doctors knew best, so we got him the shots and didn't think anything else of it. In a matter of two days we began noticing little changes in Connor. Instead of talking, he started to point when he wanted something. His eye contact in the following few weeks changed dramatically. Instead of looking us in the eyes, he would turn away.

We also noticed he wanted to play by himself in a corner of the room. Before, he loved to play with others, but now he sat alone and at times stared at the wall or off into space. In the days and weeks following, his speech stopped altogether. I cannot fully articulate how shocking it was to witness this happening to our son.

Once affectionate, Connor now showed no emotion whatsoever. And his speech began to deteriorate. Laughter and "I love you" once filled the rooms of our house, but now all we heard from him was silence. What had happened to our boy?

When our son changed, life got a whole lot more serious. Questions flooded our minds. How could we help him? Everybody had an opinion on what to do, but we didn't even have an official diagnosis. Fear was calling out to us daily.

Our family had just moved to Houston, Texas, from California to join the staff at Lakewood Church with Joel and Victoria Osteen. It was an exciting time for the church. God was raising up Pastor Joel to be a key voice in reaching people all around the world. His television ministry had skyrocketed, and his message of hope was influencing people from every socioeconomic background. People who would never go to church were watching Joel, and when he gave the salvation call at the end of the program each week, thousands made decisions to accept Jesus Christ as their personal Savior.

Shortly after we joined the church's staff in 2004, Joel's first book, *Your Best Life Now*, was released by Time Warner, debuting toward the top of the *New York Times* bestseller list and quickly rising to number one. It remained on that list for more than two years and has sold more than eight million copies—extraordinary for a first-time author.

Lakewood Church was just about to move into the former Compaq Center, where the Houston Rockets won their championships. Our team was predicting that the church would grow by twenty-five thousand people when we moved into the new facility, and that's exactly what happened. It was a historic time in our lives and the church, but it was also an overwhelming time. As crowds were coming in droves to hear the message of hope, our ministry teams completely depended on God to show us what to do; we didn't have enough volunteers and staff to handle them all.

No leadership book teaches you what to do when God is doing something that has never been done. So, instead of trying to figure it out, we just asked God, "What would You do here? How would You respond here?" Every time, even at the last minute, God would come through. I have found that if you stay faithful, God will give you just what you need when you need it.

So when Connor began to change, we were facing a perfect storm: challenges in both our work life and our home life. On one hand we were trying to figure out how to respond to our son and what the problem could be. On the other hand we were in the middle of the busiest season of our church's history.

I remember coming home from work one day to see my son was crying in frustration. I looked at my wife in her exhaustion and thought, *Where do we even start? There are so many challenges, but not enough answers.* All that I could do at that moment was say, "Peace, peace, peace."

As I said those words, I was reminded of the story in the Bible when Jesus told His disciples, as evening came, "Let's cross to the other side of the lake."

So they took Jesus in the boat and started out, leaving the crowds behind (although other boats followed). But soon a fierce storm came up. High waves were breaking into the boat, and it began to fill with water.

Jesus was sleeping at the back of the boat with his head on a cushion. The disciples woke him up, shouting, "Teacher, don't you care that we're going to drown?"

When Jesus woke up, he rebuked the wind and said to the waves, "Silence! Be still!" Suddenly the wind stopped, and there was a great calm. (Mark 4:36–39)

I've found the calm does not just come before the storm; sometimes it comes after the storm. We don't let the storm speak to us; we learn to speak to the storm. The wind may blow, but it's not our Master. God is. Maybe all we can do is say, "Peace, peace, peace," or even better, "Jesus." But the minute we begin to pray together, thoughts of doubt and fear begin to turn to peace and calm. In our case, on this evening, our son even stopped crying.

We knew there were probably some rough times ahead. But God was showing us how to manage our storm until the answer came.

This was an important early lesson. We couldn't stop every problem, difficulty, or storm from happening, but, with God's help, we could speak to it, and have peace that passed understanding. We would need this in the days ahead— especially when we got Connor's diagnosis. We knew a storm was coming.

We took Connor to Texas Children's Hospital for testing. We had an idea of what was wrong, but we still needed a diagnosis.

I was driving home from work when my wife called me on the phone with the results.

"Craig," she said, "the report just came back, and they said Connor has autism, and he is on the middle of the spectrum."

A diagnosis can seem so final—especially when there is no cure. But remember this: God always has the final word. Nothing is final unless God says it is.

Doctors explained to us that basically there are three points on the autism spectrum: high, middle, and low. If you are higher functioning, in most cases you can live independently, though you will require some support. If you are middle functioning, you have less of a chance to live independently and you will require substantial support. If you are lower functioning, you cannot live independently, and you require very substantial support. Based on that diagnosis, our son was the middle child of the spectrum.

After Sam told me the diagnosis, the Enemy began to fill me with thoughts of despair: *Your child will be your lot in life. He won't do great things like your other kids. Your child is deficient, a curse on your family. Your child has no purpose in life.*

I could feel the heaviness blanket me. In that moment I had a choice: give in to what the Enemy was saying about my boy or believe in what God said about my boy. I decided to speak declarations of hope and healing over his life. It was mind-blowing how those declarations would change the atmosphere.

As soon as I got home, instead of listening to the Enemy, I ran upstairs to Connor's room, picked him up, held him in my arms, and said, "You are not a victim; you are a victor! You are the head and not the tail! You are above and not beneath! You are more than a conqueror! You can do all things through Christ who strengthens you!" I was declaring he was a champion!

A shot of God's grace filled that room. I could feel His approval of my son with every declaration I spoke. The Enemy thought he had us down, but God was giving us the faith we needed to stand up.

There is beauty in resisting what you know to be untrue. I felt a peace that day unlike I've ever felt before or since. I also knew it was the calm before the storm.

TWO

Bend, but Don't Break

When something monumental like this happens in your life, you end one way of doing life together and begin a new normal—except it doesn't feel normal at all. It's like when you're engaged and then you finally get married. When the honeymoon is over, the real work begins. Of course, our life before autism wasn't a honeymoon all the time, but compared to after autism, let's just say life was much easier to manage. The normal things we did with our other children were not possible with Connor.

Before he changed, even at almost two years of age, Connor could ask for things he wanted. He would say, "Water, please," or "Cookies?" Now, with his speech gone, all he could do was point and grunt. This was not unfamiliar to my wife, who had experienced this type of behavior when I was watching sports on TV. She would try to talk to me, and I would just point and grunt. Maybe it runs in our family; I think my dad did that as well.

The difference, of course, was that we were being lazy.

We could still talk, but Connor couldn't. To lighten these moments, our whole family would point and grunt when we wanted something. It was hilarious. We weren't trying to poke fun at a serious situation, but sometimes we just had to find ways to release what felt so overwhelming.

At times like these, you have to learn to smile in the pain, and the greatest release of stress is laughter. Even fake laughter is better than no laughter. We often had to fake it. We weren't feeling it on the inside, but we decided to walk around expressing humor on the outside. There was a good chance that, if you had come over to our house at dinner, you would have witnessed a weird family walking around pointing and grunting—and then bursting out in laughter. It may have looked like Crazy Town to others, but it was the new normal for us.

We slowly began to tell others about Connor's diagnosis— first our family and then some of our friends. Unfortunately, many people did not know how to respond to the difficult news. They tried their best, but it just came out awkwardly.

We heard the supportive response, with words like, "We are standing with you," and "How can we come alongside you and support you?"

Then there was the "death in the family" response: "Our thoughts and prayers are with you during this difficult time. If there's anything—I mean anything—we can do, don't hesitate to call."

Sometimes we heard the "please change the subject" response, in which listeners nodded their heads, but the more you talked about it, the more they looked for an exit.

We even got the "Old Testament judgment" response—no words, just a look that said, *If you didn't have sin in your life, this wouldn't have happened.*

The "faith response" was usually, "I'm believing he is healed in Jesus' name." (Agreed. I'll have more to say on this response later.)

But the most common was the "Have you tried this?" response. People genuinely wanted to help us. They told us about TV segments on autism they watched on *Good Morning America* or *The Today Show* or different doctors they read about in magazines. They would share about the latest diet, cleanse, or other procedure. I remember the first time I heard of gluten-free foods more than a decade ago. You could only find them in a few stores then, and if you did, they were very expensive.

But we took whatever advice we could get. Early on we had to grab hold of whatever positive thing came our way and focus on it. We had tremendously difficult days when it seemed everything went wrong, but on those days we tried to say, "At least our family is healthy. Thank God we have a roof over our head and a car to drive and clothes to wear and food to eat."

We learned in this period that sometimes life is two steps forward and one step back. Even if you take a step back, you can choose to focus on the one step further you've come toward reaching your destination. The problem with us as humans is that we tend to concentrate on the one step back, not the two steps forward. If you don't learn to break it down in a positive way, you will find yourself in constant crisis mode.

How did thankfulness and positivity help us, you ask? The truth is that no matter how bad your situation is, someone out there is in a worse situation, and for that alone you have something to be thankful for—and someone else to pray for. The Enemy wants to give you a shovel and let you dig a hole of pain so deep that you can't find your way out of it. Our shovel was autism. Your shovel may be a failed marriage, financial struggles, or sickness. But we decided early on that we were not going to let autism dictate Connor's destiny. I once heard someone say that happiness is not something you are born with; it's not something you earn; it's not something given to you. Happiness is a choice. We tried every day to make that choice.

When something traumatic happens in life you may start to experience shame—especially if you think you could have done something to prevent it. You can get past denial early on, but shame comes close on its heels. The Enemy loves to build a wall of shame and put our pictures on it. Every time we see that wall, he wants to remind us of what we did wrong. It's the shame game. If you play this game with anyone, there is never a winner, and there are always losers. No matter what you go through in life, one thing is true: no one is perfect, and everyone has failed except Jesus.

Our shame during this time came from thinking that if we wouldn't have taken our son to get his vaccinations, all this would have never happened. We would never say it out loud, but early on, when the subject came up, I could see tears well up in Sam's eyes and I knew she saw her picture on the wall of shame.

It wasn't her fault or mine that this took place. It was part of a divine plan that had yet to be revealed. So the minute either one of us would feel shame, we would immediately grab hands and pray against it. A quick response can save a lot of prolonged shame from lingering. We *felt* it leave too. As quickly as the Enemy put our picture on the wall of shame, God came and took it down, replacing it with a picture of grace.

When fear comes knocking, answer the door with faith. Don't hide. Face it with confidence, knowing you are covered by the grace of God. You don't have to deny where you've been. Recover where you are.

Life often wants to break us, but when we stay faithful even in the middle of the storm, we will bend but not break if our roots are strong and deep. We can't always control what happens at the surface, but how much we get knocked down will depend on how deep our roots are.

You are stronger than you think. God has planted roots for you that, until you face major obstacles in your life, you didn't even realize were there.

When it came to finding a way to help our child developmentally, we were about to discover the "bend, but don't break" principle. We knew that early development was crucial for a child on the autism spectrum. So we began our search for schools, behavioral and language therapists, and any other kind of therapy we could find. My wife and I needed sleep therapy because our son was waking up at all hours of the night, and we would find ourselves comatose at work or sleeping with our eyes open.

We discovered some real-life challenges when it came to schools for special needs. Many public school systems will tell you they are failing in two areas: at-risk children and special needs. It's not because they have uncaring teachers who don't want to help. It's because the number of special-needs children and teens has grown so much, and the student-to-teacher ratio is so high, it is difficult for them to develop individual children effectively. You can't have a five-to-one student-teacher ratio and expect to see struggling children progress over an extended period.

A child like Connor usually needs a one-to-one or even a two-to-one student-teacher ratio to experience effective growth. So even if that child's teacher is a great teacher, and she has more than two students, she will likely struggle—and so will the child. We know this because that was our initial experience with Connor; even though he had great teachers in one of the best public school systems in Texas, after a while we saw our son begin to regress.

We started to look for private schools, most of which cost from fifteen hundred to five thousand dollars a month. That's almost as much as a Beverly Hills housewife's monthly Botox treatment! I make a good salary, but still, that's four house payments.

If you can't help your child develop effectively, what do you do?

This is the dilemma facing many parents across the world. There are millions of children and teens with special needs in America, and in my observation, many states put special-needs programs at the top of their lists when cutting education funds. I watched a single mother of a severely autistic child cry on a news program because she had finally gotten a job so she could get off welfare, but now the state was cutting its special needs funding. This affected those with severe needs, and she would now have to quit her job to go back to the home to take care of her son, which ultimately meant she would go back on welfare.

People often try to beat the system, yet here was someone who wanted to do the right thing but got beaten up by the system. We must encourage those who are doing their best to not just make it, but to jump over their mountains. When we notice someone trying to do the right thing in the face of great hurdles, we cannot just stay on the sidelines. We must come alongside them and run the race with them.

According to statistics at Disabled-World.com, approximately 15 percent of the total world's population—or roughly a billion people—live with some type of disability.[1] It's not that they need to be carried; they just need a helping hand. Those with special needs can conquer their disabilities when people unite and support one another.

We have the power to help them! They may bend, but they won't break, if we do our part. That's what fueled us to start the Champions Club at Lakewood Church—a place to help develop these children and provide hope to their families.

One night years later, after we started Champions Clubs to help families in need, I got a call from one of our club staff members. He said a man who was serving on the drama team that night wanted to meet with me. I went down to meet with the gentleman, and when I saw him, I hoped I hadn't done anything wrong—because he was huge. At six feet, four inches or so, he had the shoulders of an NFL lineman. He was staring right at me as I came down the hallway.

As I approached, his eyes began to get glassy and tear up. He said, "Are you Pastor Craig?"

I said, "Yes, sir." (That's what you say to guys who can crumple you like an aluminum can.)

"I've been wanting to meet you," he said.

I thought, *Okay, he's still talking calmly and hasn't tried to kill me yet, so things are looking up.*

Then a tear streamed down his face as this gentle giant shared a story deep from his soul. He said, "I've been wanting to meet you because I wanted to thank you."

"Thank me for what?" I asked.

"I wanted to thank you for the Champions Club you have here for special needs at the church."

He explained that his son was autistic and that their family had attended another church for many years. A few years earlier they were told that their son would not be able to come anymore. The man told them if his son could not come then he and his wife could not come either. For a year and a half they hadn't been going to church—until they heard about Lakewood. They heard there was a place at Lakewood where any child was accepted, no matter what their special need was. Their son is lower functioning and nonverbal, so when they heard this, they were amazed. When they brought him to Lakewood, everyone was loving and accepting, and they made their son and family feel welcomed. The boy had been going to the Champions Club, and the parents got to come to church and sit in a service for the first time in years.

"I just wanted to thank you," the man said, "because tonight I will be volunteering for the first time in years here at the church on the drama team. I just wanted to shake your hand and say thank-you to you and Pastor Joel for starting the Champions Club for special needs."

By the end of the conversation, we were both crying. This story is not uncommon. Probably one of the biggest tragedies of the church is that many have forgotten those with special needs. If the average church in America is made up of a hundred people, I would estimate less than 5 percent of churches in the United States have any type of program for special needs. I think I'm being generous with that figure. It could be far lower.

I recently spoke with an author friend of mine who was doing research for a book. She said she surveyed around twenty-five families with special needs and asked them to describe their most painful experience as a special-needs family. Fifty percent of them said that painful experience happened in the church. It's hard enough when families with special needs struggle with medical and developmental issues. But when they don't have a supportive spiritual environment, I can see how anyone facing those types of challenges can feel like a victim of their circumstances.

Rejection is a very hard pill to swallow. It can cause bitterness and hurt that can take a long time to heal. In most cases, churches are not excluding these families intentionally. In many cases, the leaders of these churches haven't rejected them; they've simply forgotten them. We, the modern church, have made programs more important than meeting needs. We've made service orders more important than serving others. I've been guilty of this myself. It's not that we are not doing good things. The question is whether we are doing the most important things

When Jesus walked on this earth, very little of His ministry was centered in the synagogue. The most important thing on His mind was revealing the power of His Father through healing the sick and lame, helping the poor, restoring the brokenhearted, and reaching the lost. We so often wait for them to come to us instead of passionately pursuing them.

Of course, let me be clear: it's a two-way street. If families like mine don't go to church and let leaders know they need help, then they play a part in creating this tough situation.

"I had no idea what they were going through. I just didn't know."

This is a statement I hear repeatedly when advocating for special needs with pastors, organizations, individuals, humanitarian groups, and others who can help. How is it that people with special needs have been around forever, and yet the challenges are still a mystery to most of society?

I'm sure there are many reasons behind the lack of awareness. If special needs are not the hot topic, it is easy for people to overlook them. If families are busy taking care of their child 24/7 and shut in at their homes, it's no wonder they are forgotten. It's often an "event" for them just to leave the home and go into the community. Yet, on the flipside, when families stay shut in because it's too exhausting to leave, and they are not out in the community, it's easy for someone to say, "I had no idea." I understand those cases in which the family is dealing with serious medical challenges that do not allow them to do what they would like. My heart is not to determine who has it harder or who has it easier. Instead, I want to find out how we can bridge the gap and bring more awareness so more people can understand and connect, in a positive way, with those who have disabilities.

We've always tried not to let fear and other obstacles stop us from living life and sharing about our son's amazing gifts and challenges. But it's not always been easy. For example, one day all the neighborhood kids were playing in front of our house on our street, like neighborhood kids do. At the time, Connor was about ten years old. We had always been protective of him, and I have to admit I was a little fearful of how others might treat him with his challenges. But that day Connor looked out the window, and before I knew it he was outside running and jumping around the other kids, yelling, "Yahoo!"

My first inclination was to bring him in so they wouldn't

stare at him, like any child would who didn't understand. But I waited. The Spirit of God was prompting me not to intervene. I prayed, *Please let them go on playing, or please let one of the kids be nice to him.*

It was wishful thinking; the next thing I knew every ball dropped to the ground. Everyone stopped what they were doing and just stared. My heart sank. Immediately my emotional response was to go out and bring Connor in so he could be safe and protected. But then I heard God ask, *Who are you protecting, Connor or your feelings?*

Wow! God knows how to ask the questions we don't always want to hear.

Instead of bringing my son into the house, I went out, put my arm around Connor and asked the kids if they knew what autism was. Everyone shook their heads so I began to explain to them why he reacts differently and what makes him so unique. Then something beautiful happened. Natalie, one of the more popular girls on the block, asked if she could play with Connor. Surprised, I said, "Sure." For the next thirty minutes, they played in Connor's clubhouse, and she observed Connor and interacted with him.

The next week, when I came home from work, I heard Connor in the backyard counting down, "Five, four, three, two, one, blastoff!" There he was, holding hands with Natalie, two girls on one side and two on the other side, jumping into the pool. Every boy in the neighborhood would have probably liked to be Connor at that point. He was having a blast!

Now most of the kids in our neighborhood understand

what Connor has, and they don't look at him the way they did before we came out of the house and shared his life with them. Sometimes people don't know what we're going through because we are too protective or afraid to let them know. It's safer inside the home, but if we want to see our kids grow and bring awareness to others, sometimes we need to take a chance and go outside.

We had faced a big change when we moved in 1998 from sunny Southern California to Seattle, Washington. When it rained in California, we would usually go inside. That's what you did. For the first six months living in Seattle we almost became shut-ins. We hardly ever went out to play or interact with people. Then one day I talked to a Seattle native and asked, "Don't you ever get depressed staying in because it's so cloudy and raining all the time?"

He said, "We don't stay in. We golf in the rain, play in the rain, do all sorts of things in the rain. It rains here 260-plus days out of the year. If you don't get out in the rain, you don't live life fully."

Those of us who are facing tremendous challenges can feel the same way. We may almost never get out and interact with people, so people may not even know about us. Even when things get challenging, we can live life to the fullest. Connor would have never made connections with those boys and girls if we had kept him "protected" in the house.

The more often people see us, the more conversations can take place and awareness will be raised—so that one day, instead of people saying, "I had no idea," they will say, "I know them!"

THREE

Do You Trust Me?

Trusting God is believing that He is at work, even when you can't see anything happening. And we weren't seeing anything happening with Connor. It had been a year since his diagnosis, and even though we had behavioral and language specialists working with him, he was not progressing. He still was not speaking much at all, and when he did, it was a grunt or maybe one word.

When you have a child with special needs, you tend to focus heavily on that child. We had two other children, Courtney and Cory. They knew life had changed but didn't fully know what it all meant any more than we did. I'm sure at times they felt the attention of their parents had shifted in another direction. We did our best to keep them from feeling that way, but Connor consumed so much of our time that it had to be weighing on them, though you would never have known it.

I never once heard our children complain about the situation. Oh, they could have, and they would have had every right to. Many times, when other kids were going to the mall, my children would offer to give Sam and me a respite and watch Connor. It meant so much just to be able to go out on a date or run to the store. Courtney and Cory always stepped up—and still do. Their maturity and selflessness is beyond their years.

When we found out that Connor was on the middle of the autism spectrum, Sam began to attach herself to Connor. He became her mission. She was on the Internet, reading books, searching everything she could find for ways to help our son. Moms have a natural instinct to take care of their children when something is wrong. Mothers of special-needs children will bond with a special-needs child in an even stronger way than with a typical child, but they often find themselves having to try to avoid neglecting their other children. Sam did an amazing job giving her best to Connor and giving her time to Cory and Courtney. Truthfully, I don't know how she did it.

In my experience, the challenge for parents of special-needs children is that while moms are maternal and instinctively attach themselves to the children, dads connect with their children most emotionally. When their child shows little or no emotion and stops speaking, it is very difficult for the father to connect the way he once did. He loves his child, but he's trying to figure out a new way to connect with his child again. This in turn frustrates the mom when she doesn't see in the father the same attachment she has for the child.

She looks at her husband and wonders what is wrong with him. He's looking back at her and thinking, *I'm just trying to figure out how to connect with my child again.* This can easily put a wedge in the relationship, and if they have any other issues in their marriage, such as communication or finances, it can pull them further apart. The divorce rate for marriages with special-needs children is typically higher for one simple reason: they have more issues to deal with.

The pressure of daily life can be overwhelming, and if the husband and wife can't come together and get help when they need it, that pressure can fracture the marriage.

A single mom with four boys shared with me what happened when her marriage was caught in the tug-of-war of autism. Her twins were born via C-section—both healthy boys weighing six pounds, seven ounces. She had stopped working to take care of her boys, she had no family support, and her husband had to work seven days a week to make ends meet.

The twins were growing perfectly, and she was a proud mom who always kept her doctor's appointments, making sure her children got their vaccines on time. She decided to go back to work because the family was living paycheck to paycheck in a two-bedroom apartment—the twins sharing a crib, and the older son with his own bed. That's when she noticed her babies were changing. They were getting sick more often, and she noticed that other younger kids were talking and doing things the boys had stopped doing or had never done.

She and her husband thought that maybe the twins were just slower than the rest of the kids. After they turned one, however, she knew something was not right. Taking the bottle away from them was almost impossible, and when she started to potty train them, she knew they did not understand what to do. If she left them alone and they had an accident, they would taste the feces and play with it. As the twins continued to grow, she got pregnant with her fourth son. She had to cut her work hours, and her mother stepped in to watch the twins. One day her mother mentioned that she thought the boys might have autism. It was hard to acknowledge, but the woman knew it was possible. Her husband was against investigating it; he'd had challenges as a baby but grew out of them, and he thought the twins would be fine, just as he was. Nevertheless, the worried mother got a referral to Texas Children's Hospital.

While she was waiting for an official diagnosis, the therapist suggested she put the twins in a private school where they could get help. She did exactly what was recommended, but with no support from her husband. He kept saying she was exaggerating and being overprotective with the twins and that they were going to be fine.

She was going through this all alone while her husband worked. The truth was, he had detached from them. He was embarrassed to say that his kids were not normal, so she was never able to cry with him. She also took criticism from other family members who said she was spending too much time taking care of the twins and not caring for her other two boys. The twins were having major behavioral issues and took much of her energy—especially when she was caring for them most of the time by herself. Because she was so tired, and her husband was so detached, their intimacy decreased. He used that to make her feel guilty for not being a good wife. She knew he loved the boys and her in his way. But it was hard for him to admit that they were not going to be the kids he wanted, and she was not going to be the wife he expected. There was a lot of arguing and a lot of anger. She asked her husband to buy insurance so they could get the twins help they needed, but he refused.

Finally the time came for the twins' diagnosis, and the couple went to the hospital. They were told that the boys had autism and that their minds were like the minds of three-month-old babies.

They took it hard. After leaving the hospital they went to the husband's family's house, where the family began criticizing the wife, telling her she wasn't a good mother and that she was not paying enough attention to all the boys.

On the long ride home from their house she cried, feeling like a failure as a mom and a wife. Her husband said nothing, did not hold her hand or promise they would work through the crisis together. Instead, he told her how badly she behaved in front of his family and reiterated what they had said about her.

The arguments got worse over time, until the couple finally separated for two months. He saw the boys twice but did not know how to handle them. He finally left the country, and they are not together anymore. Now she is living day to day on income that comes from the boys' Social Security checks and child support. She has a job cleaning houses for two hours a day while the boys are in school. She and her other boys mow yards, watch dogs, and help friends host dinners or parties on weekends.

It's hard to come to grips with their life without their dad, the woman says, but she clings to the promises of God and attests to the fact that He has been with them since the beginning and will not leave them.

In this case, the husband's inability to deal with autism was the wedge that drove husband and wife apart. Think of it like splitting a big block of wood—an axe isn't enough, so a wedge must be used. With every hit of the hammer the wedge begins to slowly split the once unbreakable block of wood until, with one last swing, it splits in half. One strike will not do the job. You have to swing multiple times to drive the wedge in. In the same way, the Enemy tries to chip away at marriages. He wants to drive a wedge between the husband and wife. Before you know it, trust is broken, and all that remains of what was once beautiful is split in half.

Because this happens so often in marriages of special-needs parents, we have to make a concerted effort to not only trust that God is working in the child's life, but that He's working in the marriage. And we trust each other, too, acting with the knowledge that God will bring us through. Sam and I had our issues, but we made a key agreement: never back away. Always keep moving toward each other. The more we stay together on issues, the less the Enemy can put a wedge between us. He can't hit us if we don't give him a target.

One of the most vital ways to move toward each other is to pray together. No matter what, we had to come into agreement first with God and then with each other. There is so much power in a marriage when couples learn to pray together instead of separately. Every time the Enemy would try to swing a hammer and drive the wedge between us, we would block it with prayer. The more we blocked it, the more tired the Enemy got.

When you do this, soon the Enemy must move on to someone else because he knows that no matter what he throws at you, it cannot penetrate the bond God has set between you and your spouse. It doesn't mean you're perfect or you do everything right. It just means you've learned to come together before the Enemy can pull you completely apart.

Another way to block the wedge is to let each other heal. Around the time Connor was four years old we started having special moments with him, when it seemed God had cleared the cloud over his brain and given us glimpses of the boy we knew before autism. We called them "Connor Moments." It would be like God snapped His fingers and instantly Connor would make eye contact with us or smile at us like we had seen him do a hundred times before. Before autism we had taken videos of Connor talking and playing with our dog Chelsea and looking at us and waving, saying, "I love you, Mommy and Daddy."

For Sam, watching these videos was therapeutic. I understand. Each spouse has his or her own process for working through difficulties. It's important for the other spouse to give that space and not put their spouse down because he or she doesn't respond the same way.

For me, however, watching these videos was too difficult. It brought up feelings of what might have been, and all I could handle, on top of everything else that was going on, was to take it day by day. I could never open my heart to what could be by rehashing what could have been. It's not easy to let go of what could have been. Letting go hurts, but not letting go will cost you a lot more than pain.

As we let go of what might have been, we were quickly met with the here and now. And we were about to learn about trusting God in unexpected ways.

From the time Connor was three years old to the time he was five years old, although he was growing physically, he operated as if he were two years old. Every day during those years, we tried to potty train him. No matter what method we tried, it just would not click. We had taken him swimming a few times, and we would always use diapers underneath his swimsuit in case he had an accident. We weren't worried about a number-one accident; we were worried about a number-two accident.

At one point, when he was four, he'd managed not to have an accident in the two times we'd taken him swimming, so we hoped he was learning to hold it while in the water. For us, it was a big deal. Because we were watching him all the time, and it seemed that no matter what we did, nothing changed— and then something did, and it brought a glimmer of hope.

That glimmer was gone in a blink of an eye when the third time we took him to the pool he had a major accident. When it happened, I could see the anguished look on my wife's face as everyone stared at our son. They had to shut down the pool and make everyone get out so they could clean up the mess.

When all eyes are looking at your child like he's a freak, and most everyone is wondering how his parents could have let this happen, it's very hard to explain those emotions. You're trying to help your son, and the only thing you can think is, *Let's get him cleaned up and go home so we don't ever have to experience something like this again.*

It was like stepping out in faith again, only to have the rug pulled out from under us for trying. We had to choose if we would get back up, step back out, and trust.

Just as any performer will tell you, when you put yourself out there, sometimes you bomb, and sometimes people applaud. In those moments of failure, if you don't give up, and you keep getting back up on stage, you may even get a standing ovation. But you can't get the ovation—the miracle—if you don't climb back up on that stage.

After that exasperating experience with our son, we had a choice to climb back up on the stage or to hide behind the curtain. Two days later the weather was hot, and Connor didn't want to be in the house, so my wife and I began to pray, "Please, God, help Connor to not have an accident when we go back to the pool. All we want is a good day playing with our son." Our family got back on the stage. We put on his swimsuit, took him to the pool, and hoped the same people who were there last time were not there. We watched him like a CIA surveillance team watches a suspect, in case he made any funny faces before "you know what" could happen. The end result was that we had a great day!

Why did we return to the pool after Connor had a nuclear explosion and we were so embarrassed a few days before? Sam and I figured it was a new day, and no matter how soiled (pun intended) Connor's past was, his future was spotless. In life, you have to get back out there. You can't let a crappy day (pun intended again) ruin everything. We ended up having a great time swimming, and when we got home, we gave Connor a standing ovation for not pooping in the pool. I don't know about you, but I think I'd rather look back at my life and say, "I can't believe we did that!" than say, "I wish we had done that!"

That wasn't the last time we had to get back up, of course. When Connor turned four he started to act out in ways that terrified even Sam and me. As a father, it's hard for me to share this in a book. To watch my son hurt himself when he would get frustrated, because he couldn't speak and express his feelings, was very difficult.

Even scarier was the fact that we didn't know when he was hurt because he couldn't tell us. If he fell and bumped his head, we would only know it if we saw a visible bump, mark, or bruise. He didn't express his emotions by crying, and he couldn't say where it hurt. The only way we knew he was sick was when he lay down on his bed and showed visible signs of illness. I cannot tell you how helpless we felt as parents. You want to help your child, but you don't know how. At times, this would bring my wife and me to tears.

When Connor got frustrated and acted out, he would scratch himself, bite himself, bang his head against the wall violently, or press his chin down against his fist so hard he would shake. These fits started sporadically, but by the time he was five years old, they were getting progressively worse.

One night, having finally put him to sleep after multiple episodes, my wife and I laid our heads on our pillows and looked at each other with tears rolling down our faces. That night we'd had all we could take. We cried until we couldn't cry anymore. What do you do when you have no more tears left to cry? You look up and know that God saw every tear that fell, counting them one by one so He could replace each tear with hope and each sorrow with joy.

The next morning we got up, worked out, took showers, got dressed, got Connor ready, ate breakfast, and did our devotional time. Our time with God helped us look up, even when everything within us wanted to look down. I left for work and stopped by Starbucks for a chai tea latte. (Real men drink chai tea, by the way.)

As I was going through the parking lot, a lady was driving so slowly over every speed bump that I thought, *Dear lady in front of me, it's a speed bump, not a land mine. Go!* Then further on down the road, I came to a red light that was taking forever, and out of sheer anxiety I honked at it. (By the way, that doesn't work.) At the next light, I honked again, and this time I yelled at it too! Once again, the light did nothing.

I could feel the rush of years of emotions coming to a head as I got on the freeway. I finally came to the point at which everyone who has ever been through a storm asks, "Why?" I wasn't asking God why I had my son. I loved my son. Instead, I was asking God, "Why is my son struggling so much?"

I spoke out loud to God while driving. With tears rolling down my cheeks I asked again, "Why is my son struggling so much?"

And then I heard God speak to me so clearly in my spirit, *Craig, your child is not a burden. Your child is a gift.*

It didn't register with me at first.

I said, "I know my child is a gift. I know what you're saying, but Father, he is struggling so much right now."

Again, I heard Him say, *Craig, your child is not a burden. Your child is a gift.*

This time though, I heard it louder in my heart. "What do you mean, Lord? He's struggling so badly right now."

Then, like a gentle whisper, God said, *Craig, you're looking at everything that's wrong with him. You're not looking at everything that's right.*

As I tried to wipe my tears, I spoke with a broken voice, "What do you mean, Father?"

Then God spoke clearly: *I am going to use your son to reach millions of people.*

This was hard for me to fathom. I was in a very vulnerable place. I spoke from my brokenness and asked, "How is my son going to reach millions of people? He can't even ask for a drink of water."

God asked me a question. This is the question He will ask whenever you are in a hard place and it seems there is no way out.

He asked, *Do you trust Me?*

To be honest, I didn't give Him an answer you would expect from a pastor, such as, "Oh, great God of the stars, skies, and universe, I trust You in my time of need."

Instead, I spoke from my broken heart, "Father, You're all we've got. I do trust You."

Little did I know that He was about to bring us to a breakthrough.

FOUR

Baal-Perazim: The God of the Breakthrough

Have you ever thought your life was going in one direction when suddenly it took a sharp turn? Maybe you thought your life was over, and you somehow survived a near-death experience. Perhaps it seems as if just yesterday you were living a different life, but now things have changed, and the life you once had is a distant memory.

Sometimes your situation may not make sense. That situation may be a surprise to you, but God has known about it since the beginning of time. Before God created the earth, He created your destiny. It isn't just for you; it is for all the people you will touch through your journey. He knew it would be hard, but He knew you could depend upon Him so His glory would be revealed through your circumstances. There are bigger things going on in the universe than our challenges—things that we cannot see, but that will one day be revealed to help humanity. Our job is to never quit until God reveals the miracle of His plan.

On that day when God asked me to trust Him and promised to use Connor to reach millions, I went through the morning thinking everything was about to get better. How could it not? I just talked to God. Creator of the universe. The omnipotent One. I felt Connor's worst outbursts were over now. It couldn't get any worse with Connor, could it?

Yes, it could; and yes, it did.

We went into autism Defcon 1 mode. We were at war! Every day it was something different. The screaming, the self-scratching, banging of his head, biting, and crying for no reason were happening all the time. Some mornings we would walk into our five-year-old's room and find him there with feces all over the floor, walls, and somehow even on the ceiling fan. In the Johnson house the crap had literally hit the fan.

On a positive note, one time we discovered that he had written his name on the wall with it. We can laugh about it now, but believe me—no one was laughing then. It was painful to watch, and the smell was so bad our dog came by his room, sniffed, shook her head in disbelief, and then sniffed her own butt. I guess it smelled better.

It's in times like these we learned that you have to do a few things just to stay sane. We were learning to laugh more, even in these extreme situations. You might be asking, "How could you laugh in the middle of that chaos?" It was better than the alternative: crying. The Bible says, "The Lord is my strength and shield. I trust him with all my heart. He helps me, and my heart is filled with joy. I burst out in songs of thanksgiving" (Ps. 28:7). In other words, the joy of the Lord is my strength. When you have no more strength within yourself to cope, why not let out a smile or chuckle, or just laugh like a crazy person? I'd rather die laughing than live crying.

We also learned to keep praying and keep pressing on. When it seems like the worst is happening, don't give up. Keep swinging. Realize what you do have, not what you don't have. Trust God. Even when every fiber of your being tells you *no*, let that last ounce of hope left inside of you be your *yes*. While we were walking through our storm, we laughed, even when it hurt, and just kept believing for our miracle.

And then it happened.

"Craig! Craig! Get up here!" I heard Sam yelling from Connor's upstairs bedroom. I thought something was seriously the matter, so I put down my book and ran upstairs as fast as I could.

"What is it?" I asked.

"I was praying with Connor before bedtime when suddenly he began to speak," she said, with tears in her eyes.

Puzzled, I asked, "What do you mean he began to speak?"

Remember, we hadn't heard our son put four words together in three years.

"He began to speak, saying one word after another word, one sentence after another sentence—a whole paragraph," she replied.

I couldn't believe what she was saying to me, and tears welled up in my eyes.

I hadn't seen this coming.

"What did he say?" I asked, grabbing my phone to capture it on film, in case he spoke again.

My wife took me by the hand, walked me over to Connor's bedside, and leaned down to speak to him.

"Say it, son. Say it again for Mommy and Daddy," she asked him.

My son slowly lifted up his head and said: "This is my Bible. I am what it says I am. I have what it says I have. I can do what it says I can do. Today I will be taught the Word of God. I boldly confess, my mind is alert, my heart is receptive, and I will never be the same. I am about to receive the incorruptible, indestructible, ever-living seed of the Word of God. I will never be the same, never, never, never, I will never be the same, in Jesus' name, amen!"

Those were the first words and sentences Connor had spoken in three years. It was unreal. A rush of joy—or, I should say, euphoria—came over my wife and me in a way we had never experienced. Have you ever laughed and cried at the same time? It's an ecstatic feeling, isn't it? That is exactly what we were doing as we hugged our son, who couldn't figure out what we were so excited about. He was ready to go to bed after all that work talking for the first time in a long time.

At nine o'clock on that Tuesday evening we got Connor out of bed, brought all the kids in, and had a dance party right in his bedroom. We were praising God, doing the hokey pokey, the running man, and the electric slide all in one. Let's put it this way: I don't think we would have been invited to be on *Dancing with the Stars* that night, but we didn't care. We were dancing for the main Star, God almighty, who brought our son back to us.

A couple of weeks later I was speaking on a Wednesday night at Lakewood Church, and I showed the crowd a video of Connor speaking for the very first time in a long while. At our church we cry a lot—not tears of sadness, but tears of gratefulness because of the goodness of God. As the congregation watched the video of Connor's miracle, Pastor Joel, who was sitting on the front row, welled up with tears of joy as he watched the miracle with his own eyes. You see, he and Victoria and the entire staff at Lakewood Church had walked with us along this journey from the very beginning.

When Sam and I felt helpless, we clung to messages of hope that we heard repeatedly from Pastor Joel and Victoria during our dark times. Families with special-needs children know what they are up against. They are just looking for some hope each week. These hope brokers—Pastor Joel and Victoria—were put in our lives when we needed them most. We replayed their messages in our minds when times got rough.

John Osteen, Pastor Joel's father and the founder of Lakewood, used to say, "Put God's Word in you when you don't need it so it will come out of you when you do need it." That's true of encouraging words too. During that three-year period, we often heard Pastor Joel speak the Word of God and give us messages like, "You're not a victim; you're a victor. You can do all things through Christ who strengthens you. You are the head and not the tail. You are above and never beneath. You are more than a conqueror. Don't look at what's wrong in your life; look at what's right."

We would hide those words in our hearts and remember them when we needed them most. Whenever we needed Pastor Joel and Victoria and the church, they came alongside us like heroes, never asking what was in it for them, only wanting what was best for us. It was like God put them in our path to help us walk it.

A few weeks after my talk, Pastor Joel preached a message called "Living Breakthrough Minded." In it he talked about the time King David was facing a monumental battle with the Philistine army (2 Sam. 5). David and his men were greatly outnumbered, and the odds were against them. David prayed and asked God to give them victory in an impossible situation. As they went out to fight this huge army, God gave them victory. Later, David said, "God has broken through my enemies by my hand, like a bursting flood" (1 Chron. 14 ESV). When they left, David named that place *Baal-Perazim*, which means essentially, "God of the breakthrough."

As Pastor Joel continued his message he talked about living breakthrough minded:

A breakthrough is a sudden burst of God's favor, an explosion of His goodness. God can release His power in such a way that you are overwhelmed and flooded with victory and answers to your prayers. When things are difficult and don't look like they are going our way, that's when it's easiest to lose our joy, vision and enthusiasm, to believe that things will never get any better. But during those challenging seasons in life we have to learn to do just the opposite. Right in the midst of the adversity, that's the time—more than ever—to expect a flood of His favor, a flood of healing, a flood of vindication, a flood of protection. Our attitude should be, "It may be dark, but I know the God of the breakthrough is about to turn things around!"[1]

I remember sitting there on the front row with Sam and Courtney, tears rolling down our cheeks, taking in every word like it was just for us. We knew exactly what David felt like. Our situation seemed hopeless, but we just kept believing. It was dark at times. Some days we felt as if we had fallen into the bottom of a well with darkness all around us, but we were hoping that someone would shine a light.

Then Joel shared the story of our son Connor. He said,

I love the story that our children's pastor told not long ago. Craig and Samantha have a son named Connor. He's a very handsome, fun little boy. Connor has autism, and he's never spoken a full paragraph. Really, he doesn't speak in sentences. He will speak a few words here and there, but day after day Craig and Samantha keep speaking favor into Connor, telling him he's more than a conqueror, that he can do all things through Christ. Every night at bedtime either Craig or Samantha will read two or three books with little Connor and then they will pray together and go to bed. The other night, just as Samantha was about to turn out the light in Connor's room, she heard him start speaking. He went on and on.

As Joel spoke, overwhelmed by what God had done, his voice began to crack. He continued, "He went on and on so clearly, so fluently, she ran and got Craig and the video camera and captured the first real paragraph he had ever spoken. This is what he was saying."

Then the video played, showing Connor saying the declaration, "This is my Bible . . ." Pastor Joel bent over at the pulpit, weeping as he listened to Connor speak. This is something most people didn't see because that thirty-minute message was edited for TV. But I can't tell you how many times I've watched Joel break down and cry in the middle of a message. He cries for hurting and broken people. He cries, filled with hope that God would give those who watch the same favor God has given him. He cries when he talks about family or stories of how people have overcome despite their circumstances. I've never in my life seen someone so broken for the human condition who believes that God can do anything, no matter what family they have come from, what circumstances they come out of, or what mistakes they have made.

The video finished, and Joel continued:

Those were his first real sentences and paragraphs. What was that? That was the God of the breakthrough visiting their house. Like a flood God's favor came upon little Connor, a flood of healing, a flood of restoration, a flood of wisdom. Now Craig and Samantha have another Baal-Perazim. That's a night they will never forget.

As he said this, I was sitting there bawling like a baby—doing the "ugly cry." You know, that cry you only hope family will never see in your lifetime? As I was doing the ugly cry, the camera panned around right to me and caught my face. It probably scared a few children. I was trying to keep it together, but it was not working because years of emotion were coming out.

It's funny—I never used to cry like I do since I've become a special-needs parent. It breaks you in a good way, and you are never the same again. You're broken and spilled out, and any moment that touches you can bring the tears.

I frequently ask Sam, "Why do I cry all the time?"

"That is God using you to cry for the things that break His heart and bring Him joy," she says. "You're His vessel."

Everyone who has been broken in life is like a vase with a crack in it. No matter how much you pour in that vase, it can never get filled up. The cracks in us allow God's grace to pour out. This brokenness is not a bad thing. Quite the contrary—it may be the best thing that can happen to someone.

I heard a story about Chuck Colson, the man who started Prison Fellowship Ministries and worked in President Nixon's administration in the sixties and seventies. Chuck's daughter, Emily, discovered her son had autism. When Chuck found out about the diagnosis, he was heartbroken, and gradually he began to share the news with a few close friends. One told him: "You have found favor from God, because he has given you this special-needs child so you can experience sacrificial love."[2]

It's true. You love differently than you once did. It's deeper because every day you learn to love without expecting anything in return.

When we told our son we loved him, we never got a response back. No feeling, no words, no reciprocation. We just loved him because he was our son. It reminds me of the sacrificial love Christ gave us. He gave His life knowing He might not get anything in return from us. He just did it because He loved us. That is sacrificial love. That is the stuff heroes are made of—ordinary people doing extraordinary things that most people would not do, all because of love.

As I listened to Pastor Joel give his message that day, talking about our son's miracle, I was reminded of the times Sam and I felt like giving up. Why didn't we? We are no different from anyone else who has gone through something like this. We have seen marriages break apart and good moms and dads victimized by their circumstances. We understand fully how that can happen. Why did we keep believing?

It wasn't that we had it all together. Our faith was constantly challenged. We just would not let hope die. Every day we kept doing a little extra. Faith doesn't make things easy; it makes them possible. Our motivator was God's unconditional love given to us despite our circumstances. His sacrificial love for us was the example we needed to help us sacrificially love our son, even when we didn't necessarily get anything in return.

As Joel continued to share our story in his talk, he said,

The night Connor spoke was a night they will never forget. Even though little Connor doesn't speak perfectly yet, they know he is well on his way. What God started He will finish. How it happened is that Craig and Samantha take the DVDs of my messages home, and little Connor will put them in and watch. They said that normally when he's watching cartoons, he'll only watch for five or ten minutes, but he'll sit there all through the day and watch my thirty-minute messages. I told Craig later, when a five-year-old chooses me over Barney, I know I have favor. But I love the fact that God gave them something to talk about. They were so excited about it, they tell everybody what God has done for little Connor. It was dark, but the light came bursting in.

We knew we had our Baal-Perazim. Our breakthrough had come. When that message aired, more than forty million people saw it in one month. The video went all around the globe, and we started getting e-mail messages from across the United States and countries all over the world. One person who oversaw special-needs schools in Cambodia sent the video to every teacher and every parent in his organization. It affected them so much they sent a letter of thanks for the inspiration our son Connor was to everyone at the schools and all the families of the special-needs children. They sent Connor two T-shirts; one said "Overcomer," and another said "Conqueror." We started getting e-mails and letters from parents of special-needs kids, saying that after they'd watched our son's miracle, they felt that if God could do it for Connor, He could do it for their child.

People who watched in the service were so affected, they wanted to see how they could help and serve kids with special needs at our church. One family after another with special-needs children would call or stop us and say how God used our son to help them not give up on their circumstances. They now could see their child had a purpose just as Connor did.

I will never forget a Lakewood event in 2011 called A Night of Hope, held at the Chicago White Sox's stadium, when they played our son's testimony in front of forty-five thousand people, and Samantha and I walked out on the field with Connor. As we walked onto the grass of the infield, Connor waved at the crowd. I looked up in the stands and saw thousands of people crying and clapping as they watched his miracle on the jumbotron video screens.

As we were experiencing this on the field, I heard God

speak to me the same way He did when I had asked Him, "Why?" in the car. He said, *Remember when you asked Me "Why?" and I told you I was going to use your son to reach millions of people? Look at all these people in this stadium and around the world who have heard his testimony. Look at them crying and clapping for little Connor. I told you if you trusted Me, I would do this. I always stay true to My word.*

Chills ran down my spine as I realized that what God said He would do, He did—and would keep doing. This wasn't the end; it was only the beginning. I knew the struggle wasn't over for us, but if we depended on God, He would finish what He started. When we found out Connor had autism, one way of life ended and a new one began. It wasn't what we thought would happen, but God was using our son, at five years old, to impact the world. It was our Baal-Perazim.

When you create a recipe for the perfect life, things may turn out different from what you originally planned. Beauty comes through the struggles, triumphs, challenges, joys, sorrows, and hopes all combined to make your perfect mess a beautiful life!

FIVE

God Is Near to the Brokenhearted

When tragedy strikes, it's time to live through the "whys" to get to the "why nots." Our son had autism, and we asked *why*. But now he has influenced so many people, and we ask, in the power of God, why not? Maybe you lost everything you had financially, but God restored more than you had before. *Why not?* You made a mistake that brought you disgrace, but God turned it around and brought you a new destiny. *Why not?* Your marriage fell apart, but God brought it back to life when it seemed like there was no hope. *Why not?* Nothing is impossible for Him.

The hardest part is working through the whys—the grief over something that has gone wrong. Many times we focus on what has happened, never thinking about what God could do through these events. Many people get discouraged and stop trying before they reach the finish line. A key is to not hold on to things we can't change. It's a shame to sacrifice all the good things that could happen in our lives for the one thing we can't change.

There is always a bigger plan. I know we don't want to hear it when we are going through the hard times. I never liked hearing my parents say, "One day you will understand." But almost all the time they were exactly right. You can't know what you haven't experienced. A doctor cannot bring healing to the patient without the knowledge, experience, and tools to help them. In the same way, we cannot help bring healing to others if we haven't walked through the broken places with God. Our experience gives us the knowledge and tools to be healers for other people. Before Jesus' crucifixion He did many great things, but it wasn't until His blood was shed and His body was broken that He could save the world.

When people are brokenhearted and don't understand what's happening to them, God draws near to them. When people fail, He draws near to those who are broken and need to be fixed.

I could never have envisioned, during that time of brokenness when our lives shifted with the news of our son, that we would go in this direction, but nothing is a surprise to God. He had it planned all along. We may have thought it was all a coincidence, but I've heard it said that coincidence is God's way of reminding us He's always there. He was about to show us a new vision for our lives.

One day I was walking through our church, looking at the graphics on the walls of our children's facilities. Suddenly I heard God speak to me, deep down in my spirit.

Craig, look at your children's facility for typical children, He said. *It looks like Disneyland with all the rooms, animation, graphics, and equipment. Now look at what you're doing for special-needs children.*

As I looked around, I saw that we were like other churches, most of which didn't have anything for special needs. We had one room with some caring individuals as instructors, and about ten special-needs participants who ranged from kids to adults.

God then said, *Look at what you are doing for typical kids, and look at what you are doing for special-needs kids. There's no comparison.*

Then He said something that I'll never forget: *Special-needs kids deserve the very best, just like every other child.*

My eyes got big because I knew we weren't doing our best for all children at our church. We were just doing our best for those who were easier to help.

It's always easier to help the ones who are front and center. But for profound change, we must be willing to do the hard things to reach all people, especially those who are hard to see and reach. When you're cleaning your house, for instance, you can clean the visible areas, but it doesn't mean your house is clean. It's not until you see and clean the hard-to-reach spaces that your house becomes truly spotless.

Shannon Dingle, a special-needs blogger for Key Ministry and a special-needs parent herself, wrote a post titled, "Don't

Tell Me Your Church's Theology Is Sound If My Family Isn't Welcome." In it she reminds us:

> If your church is hearing the word but not putting it into action, then the Bible says you're fooling yourself. And if you say you love your city but you're willing to say no to people with disabilities—even knowing that nearly 20 percent of Americans have a disability, half of whom report their disability as severe, according to the 2010 US Census—then you're deceiving yourselves.
>
> I'm not saying every church needs to put in place supports for every imaginable disability area. Our church, with a well-established special needs ministry, certainly doesn't have that! I wouldn't expect any new church to be fully equipped with how to support our family if we wanted to join. But I would expect, hope, wish, pray, that they would be willing to love us enough to try to learn.[1]

I concur with Shannon. You can't say you're a church that wants to reach hurting people if you're only willing to help certain types of hurting families and not others. When the need is so big, with more than fifty million people with disabilities in America alone, something needs to change. I believe the church needs to reevaluate why they pick and choose whom they are comfortable helping.

If we think the church doesn't discriminate based on race, gender, and ability, we're kidding ourselves. We all carry the responsibility for the fact that we have missed the mark when it comes to whom we cater to and whom we leave out. We must move from the selective church to the inclusive church. God is near to *all* the brokenhearted, and maybe it's time for the church to remember the ones God never forgets.

When I went into the one classroom our church had for special needs, tears filled my eyes. I heard God speak to me again: *When you look into the eyes of a person who has special needs, you are looking at Me. It's My reflection, because when you do it unto the least of these, you are doing it unto Me.*

I had never thought of it that way—that it's as if God were standing next to me, and I were serving Him through these children. Then God spoke one last thing: *Favor will follow those who reach the least of these.*

So many people are looking for favor from people rather than from God. Human nature says to pursue people of influence. That makes sense. There's nothing wrong with learning and growing from time with influential people. I've had that privilege in my lifetime. It's always an honor. The caveat is, if you become motivated by the favor of people more than the favor of God, you're on a slippery slope that often ends in disappointment.

There will always be a price to pay for favor from man, but when you are a child of God, you are already in a place of favor. God will give you a road map to His divine favor and blessings. All you have to do is follow it.

When God said, *Favor will follow those who reach the least of these*, I was reminded of a passage in the Bible in Luke 14, when Jesus went to eat dinner at the home of the leader of the

Pharisees. All the people there were watching him closely. When Jesus noticed that all who had come to the dinner were trying to sit in the seats of honor near the head of the table, He gave them this advice:

> When you are invited to a wedding feast don't sit in the seat of honor. . . . Instead, take the lowest place at the foot of the table. Then when your host sees you, he will come and say, "Friend, we have a better place for you!" . . . For those who exalt themselves will be humbled, and those who humble themselves will be exalted. (vv. 8–11)

But as He continued, I saw where favor follows:

> Then he turned to the host. "When you put on a luncheon or a banquet," he said, "Don't invite your friends, brothers, relatives, and rich neighbors. For they will invite you back, and that will be your only reward. Instead, invite the poor, the crippled, the lame, and the blind. Then at the resurrection of the righteous, God will reward you for inviting those who could not repay you." (v. 12)

There's nothing wrong with pursuing people of influence, but you may get back only what their influence can pay you. You cannot compare the influence and favor of man to that of God. God says if you want His favor, pursue the least of these. I believe if you want influence, you chase after what moves God, not what moves man.

I've seen people push through crowds, wait hours in line, or even pay money to get a picture with someone famous. On the surface, there is nothing wrong with that. But what if we got just as excited taking a picture with someone who was poor, disabled, unpopular, broken, a person of no reputation? You may not get the same response from your friends and family, but God would say, "Wow! How cool was that? I love them!" And He would not stop there; He repays far beyond what man can repay. The Bible says He owns the cattle on a thousand hills (Ps. 50:10). God might say, "How can I bless them? What can I do for My child who has pleased me so much by remembering those who need it the most?"

We had no idea how much of God's favor and influence was with us. I didn't know how to effectively develop a program for kids and families with special needs, and I hadn't seen many examples in churches. But God began to show us how to create what would become our first Champions Club. We never would have thought of it without Him.

First we searched out key people to be a part of our task force to develop a special-needs ministry that wouldn't just take care of the kids but would help them develop at different levels. For too long these children and their families had been an afterthought, and I wanted them to feel that in our ministry they were the only thought. We needed to give them the best, so I looked for top experts in the community to help us learn what the best would look like.

I wanted this team to cover four areas of expertise in special needs: research, educational, spiritual, and parenting from people who themselves were parents of special-needs children. God was leading us toward a holistic approach.

In 2007 I first came across three amazing doctors: Jair Soares, Katherine Loveland, and Deborah Pearson—all of whom were at the University of Texas Medical Center doing some ground-breaking research for special-needs children. I saw them on our local ABC station in Houston while they were recruiting potential families to participate in their research. We thought Connor might make a good candidate for their study, so we took him in and let them observe him. To be honest, I had two motives: to help my son and to ask if they would meet with me to discuss becoming a part of the task force. Fortunately, they took the meeting and let me share my heart about our program. They agreed to come onboard, and our task force was on the way to becoming a reality.

I then looked for an educator who would understand curriculum and development for the program, and we found Dr. Charles Meisgeier, founding chairman of the Department of Special Education at the University of Houston. He also agreed to be a part of our task force.

For our spiritual focus, we pulled together some of the top team members in our children's and family ministry at Lakewood Church who had expertise in ministry and development. Then we brought in some of the most valuable resources you could ever have in this situation: the parents of special-needs children. They are the ones walking the journey day by day, giving their best to see their children become everything they were meant to be.

Once we had the team in place, we knew we could begin to develop the program, but the most important person was missing. I still needed someone to run the program.

I needed a giant of faith on whose shoulders these kids and families could stand. I also felt I needed someone with expertise in the field of special needs to lead the program—someone who had a passion and a heart for these children.

One person on my staff wasn't an expert in this area but was a great administrator and leader. She had been working with our children's ministry both as a volunteer and on staff for years, and she was outstanding. She had given up a high-paying job running the office of a law firm to come on staff, but for years she had also worked diligently as a volunteer, serving and loving children.

Whenever I talked to Norma Puga about our son or other children with special needs, tears would come to her eyes. God spoke to me and said, *She's the one. Don't worry about her expertise, because her heart and excellence are second to none. These children and families need to be loved and accepted more than anything else. She will be My instrument to do that.*

I knew I had heard from God, and I was hoping Norma had heard from God too. One day we sat down with her and told her what we were planning to do, asking if this was something she would be interested in. Without hesitation, while tears rolled down her cheeks, she said, "Yes." I think I shouted, "Yes!" as well. We had our task force, we had our leader, and now we needed God to guide us toward what our program would become.

It took one year to develop what would ultimately be called the Champions Club. We were already using that name in the limited program we already had for special-needs children, and I loved it. No need to fix what wasn't broken. During our developmental meetings, we discovered that we needed tools to keep the children engaged and to help the leaders teach. As I've said, we wanted to see these kids developed, not just babysat.

And we wanted a program that supported parents as well as kids. That meant that when the parents showed up, we would give them special attention and care and make them feel like the most important parents in the church. We also wanted to create support for the parents through respite events, small groups for special-needs families, and camps and events for the entire family. They were carrying a heavy load, but we knew if we could come alongside them, that load could be lifted, even if only for a couple of hours. We also wanted them to trust the excellence of our program so they would not worry and would feel free to go to church, possibly for the first time in years, hear an uplifting message, and participate in a community of faith.

We also wanted to make sure our program was compre-
hensive enough that no child would ever be turned away, no
matter what their special need was, and no matter how severe
it was. We wanted them to experience love and acceptance
like they had never experienced it before. We wanted to
make it our mission that, for at least two hours of the week,
their child would get the best care, and they as parents could
experience a service with no interruption so they could receive
the encouragement and hope they needed to make the coming
week their best week yet.

Being turned away or having to leave is something that is
an all too common experience for a special-needs family. We
had experienced that pain many times, especially when we
tried to put our son in a local private school that was highly
recommended for special-needs children. When Connor was
seven years old, we applied and hoped. But when my wife
met with the assistant principal, she heard, "I'm sorry, Mrs.
Johnson, but we can't accept your son Connor into the school.
We only accept higher functioning students, and although
Connor meets the academic requirements, he doesn't quite
meet the social side."

Though dreadfully disappointed, my wife could ultimately accept that this was a school for a certain type of
special need, although she didn't think that was fair. What she
couldn't accept was the next part of their conversation.

"What should we do to help our son?" Sam asked. "And can you help us find another option?"

"I'm not sure, but he won't be able to come here," the assistant principal replied. "You'll just have to find a school that will accept him."

Now, my wife is one of the sweetest and kindest people you will ever meet, but Momma Bear was about to growl.

"If you're going to call yourselves a special-needs school, then be a school for all the kids and their challenges, not just the easier cases," she said. "And another thing—you should never say what you just said to me as a special-needs parent. When people walk away from your school, they should feel hope, not despair."

Later, when Sam was telling me the story, she exclaimed, "Craig, we need to start a school of our own! We could create a school where no child or parent is turned away."

I said, "Now hold on, honey, I know you're upset, but with everything on my plate, I'm not sure if starting a school is on the menu."

Then she said something I'll never forget.

"You should never leave a place that says they bring hope, without hope."

That statement kept ringing in my head. If you are a place that is supposed to bring hope, no one should ever walk away without a taste of it.

That very day God spoke to me and said, *I want you to start Champions Clubs in churches in the north, south, east, and west. I also want you to start Champions Academy schools for special-needs children. Match up a Champions Club in a church with a Champions Academy school in the same area. If there is no room at the school, they can always go to the Champions Club in a church nearby until there is an opening. This way, no matter what, they will be able to go to one or both, but they will never be turned away without hope.*

We made it our mission to never turn away a child and to always make sure the family left with hope.

In March 2008, the Champions Club became a reality at Lakewood Church. It was an unprecedented, specially designed developmental area for kids, youth, and adults with special needs, focused on ministering to them spiritually, intellectually, sensorily, and physically. We reached for spiritual growth through God's Word, developing the intellect of each participant through the five senses, and engaging the child physically during active gross motor fun. We designed Champions Clubs to be adapted to any school or public facility environment, and would eventually be proud to see Champions Clubs in schools, churches, and facilities across America and around the world.

The weekend we announced the Champions Club, one month before the opening date, I shared with the congregation of Lakewood, knowing my words were reaching more than forty thousand people online and across the campuses of our church. "I know many of you special-needs families are not here today," I said, "but you are shut in, watching online from your home. Many of you have felt rejected by society and rejected by churches. You feel forgotten. We have worked for almost a year to build a program and state-of-the-art rooms that will allow you to come to church for the first time, volunteer, and be a part of a community while your children are getting the best care and development. I know you've felt forgotten, but you're not forgotten anymore."

As I finished, the crowd in each service rose to their feet and roared for these children and families. I will never forget a mother of a severely autistic child saying, with tears in her eyes, "This is the greatest thing anyone has ever done for me and my child. You didn't forget us, and you gave us your best. We're not forgotten anymore."

When we started, we had five volunteers, plus our director, Norma, and we had to recruit enough staff to cater to congregants in seven different services in Spanish and in English. We needed a miracle! That first weekend, we gave the congregation the opportunity to tour the Champions Club before it opened. If they had the heart to serve in this ministry, they could sign up, and we would train them.

That weekend a miracle happened, and we had 175 applications. More than half of them had experience in different areas of special needs. Remember what God told me? *Favor will follow you when you reach the least of these.* It did! We didn't even know these qualified people were in our congregation.

After we opened the doors one month later, more than three hundred families came to Lakewood Church to experience the Champions Club during the following six months. God met all our needs and even went above and beyond. We learned in an amazing way that favor will follow when you reach the least of these, because God is truly near to the brokenhearted.

SIX

Standing on the Shoulders of Giants

When I played football in high school, we used to have dinners on Thursday nights before the Friday games. One Thursday, the family who hosted the dinner had a pool, so we all jumped in. We used to have what were called chicken fights. In a chicken fight, you climb on the shoulders of a person in the pool and wrestle the other person who is on the shoulders of another opponent. The one who knocks his opponent off his partner's shoulders first wins. In my first chicken fight I was on the shoulders of one of our receivers. He was tall and lanky with skinny feet and legs. When they yelled, "Go!" our opponent knocked my partner and me backward because the receiver just wasn't strong enough to hold us both up.

Well, in the next round I got smart. I climbed on the shoulders of a giant. His name was Muli Muli Malauli. He was a Samoan with big feet, legs that looked like logs, and shoulders that simulated a brick wall. He was big and strong—and one of the nicest guys you would ever meet, unless he was competing against you. I knew when I climbed on his shoulders, I had a champion. No one was going to knock me off.

Sure enough, when we got into the water and I climbed up on his shoulders, I felt stronger already. They yelled, "Go!" and the chicken fight battle royale began. Our opponents came at us, but they couldn't knock me off Muli's shoulders. He held on to my legs and would not let go. We overpowered everyone. He planted those big feet on the bottom of the pool, I would wrestle the opponent, and even if he was bigger than me, Muli could not be moved. We won every battle because of Muli Muli. I was standing on the shoulders of a giant.

Isaac Newton said, "If I have seen further it is by standing on the shoulders of giants."[1] As I am writing this, I believe I am talking to just such a giant—a hero. You might be saying, "Who, me? I've never done anything heroic in my life. I'm lucky to be here." Trust me. Anyone can be a giant. Today you may feel invisible, but one day you will be invaluable.

There is usually one common thread in stories of heroes: they never consider themselves to be heroes. They were unsung people whom God put in the right position at the right time to do something heroic. Hebrews 11, the "Heroes of the Faith" chapter, describes ordinary people who did extraordinary things. Hebrews 11:1–2 says, "Faith means being sure of the things we hope for and knowing that something is real even if we do not see it. Faith is the reason we remember great people who lived in the past" (NCV).

This chapter of the Bible remembers these people as giants of the faith—not because they were born heroic. They weren't. They were normal people like you and me, and some had bigger flaws than you or I have. David was an adulterer and murderer. Peter was a liar who denied Christ. Paul persecuted Christians and had them killed. Rahab was a prostitute, but she became one of God's heroes when she hid and protected the men who came to spy on Jericho. God used them all mightily because He saw something inside them no one else could see. He saw their faith.

They weren't heroes because they were perfect. They were heroes because of their faith. Even in their weakest moments they found the faith to keep going and not give up. They had the faith to trust God, even when no one else believed in them. God never asks if you are qualified to respond; He just asks if you are willing. And if He lifts you up, you can achieve anything.

When a giant of a man named Goliath came to destroy the army of Israel, all the physically strong and mighty warriors, including the king, stood there like scared little children in his presence. Physically he was huge. He stood ten feet tall, and he could wear armor that weighed 126 pounds. He held a spear that looked like a fence rail, and the tip of the spear alone weighed 15 pounds. How would you like to carry that around on your way to a fight?

The interesting thing is that when Goliath called out to all these mighty warriors to fight him, not one of them had the courage to accept his challenge. They had two disadvantages in this battle. First, they thought this was a physical battle, not a supernatural battle. Physically they had no chance of winning, but supernaturally they had no chance of losing. Second, they had the wrong vantage point. They were looking up at the giant. When you look up at your problems, they can seem overwhelming, but when you look down at your problems, from a higher point of view, they will seem miniscule.

Most things in life are about perspective. Goliath was a giant of a man, but he wasn't a giant of the faith. When little David showed up and told the king he would fight against this gigantic Philistine, he was either crazy or he was walking in supernatural strength. Heroes will rise when they are confident they are standing on the shoulders of Almighty God. David saw Goliath from a totally different perspective.

Giants of the faith are not giants because of their stature. They are giants because of their confidence in God. You have a boldness you never had on your own. You feel empowered to aim high and think big. Isaiah 40:29–31 says,

> He gives power to the weak
> > and strength to the powerless.
> Even youths will become weak and tired,
> > and young men will fall in exhaustion.
> But those who trust in the Lord will find new strength.
> > They will soar high on wings like eagles.
> They will run and not grow weary.
> > They will walk and not faint.

David knew he wasn't a hero, but he was made by a Hero—the greatest Superhero of all, God Himself. David was made in His image, like all of us. Heroism ran in his veins. The Enemy tries to trick us into believing we aren't from the same bloodline as the Creator of the universe, that we are incapable of doing anything heroic.

But God says, "If you can't stand on your own, I will provide the shoulders you can stand on—My own, and even those of someone I send. Then I will use you to help others. Through your testimony others will then stand on your shoulders and be able to see farther than they have ever seen before."

David climbed on God's shoulders that day and defeated a giant with a slingshot and five stones. David may have been small, but that day he felt a thousand feet tall. Then God used him to become a giant of the faith for an entire nation.

You may say, "Craig, I'm going through so many storms in my life. How can I help someone else? How can I serve as a giant for others?"

Don't forfeit your power by being overwhelmed by your circumstances. We all face storms in our lives. Some are small, and some are huge. But again, it's how we respond to the storms that matters.

Too many times we let our storms speak to us rather than taking authority over the situation like Jesus did. You don't even have to come up with your own words when you're going through a storm. Just say His words, "Peace, be still!" (Mark 4:39 NKJV). You can either speak to your storm, or hide from your storm.

How do we speak to our storms without fear? Here is a key concept I would love for you to absorb deep in your spirit. This is one you can highlight and go back to every time you're going through a challenge in your life. I've found that when I'm going through a storm, the best thing I can do is *be good to someone else*. It takes my mind off my difficulties, and it brings understanding that this storm was not meant to destroy me. It was meant to take me higher.

When we begin to help others go higher, to offer our shoulders as we stand on God's shoulders and on the shoulders of the giants in His Word, even in the midst of our storms, we will begin to look at life from a different vantage point. Our problems won't look so overwhelming anymore. They may even lead us to our new mission in life. I never thought my mission in life would be to help those with special needs, but my storm brought me to my greatest purpose.

Even on your worst day you may become someone else's best hope. In the Bible, again, God didn't use people who had it all together. He used people who were willing to take the little they had and give it to God. We don't need to have it all together either. He uses the most unlikely people to become giants of the faith in someone else's life.

Take my father, for instance. He was always a hard-working man. When he was sixteen, he felt called to the ministry. In those days most pastors couldn't support themselves on a minister's salary, so my dad pastored the church on weekends and moved furniture for Bekins Van Lines during the week to make ends meet. My mother worked odd jobs to bring in extra money. They didn't have a lot, but they were happy to be together. They had only been married a year and a half when they had their first child, Radonda.

When my sister, Radonda, was born, she was born with no kneecaps. Her legs would bend forward instead of backward, to the point where she could touch the top of her forehead with the tips of her toes. The medical term for it was *skeletal dysplasia*. By the time she was almost two years old, she had two major surgeries and two minor surgeries on her little legs. Before the last surgery my father and mother were brought into the doctor's office and told, "I'm sorry, Mr. and Mrs. Johnson, we have done all that we can do, but your daughter will probably never walk again."

My father and mother began to cry and walked out of the hospital room, heartbroken for their baby girl. As they were driving home from the hospital in Tulare, California, my father was so distraught, he told my mother he was going to step away from the ministry. He said it was too hard to keep going in ministry and take care of a disabled child, plus work another job. At that time, my dad and mom were just twenty years old.

My sister was in a body cast that went from her ankles all the way up to her armpits. The idea that she would never walk again was heartbreaking for my parents. Their whole world seemed like it had stopped in front of them. My mom tried to encourage my dad to wait before he made any rash decisions, but my father was at such a vulnerable place in his life that his brokenness overwhelmed him. All he could think of was how he was going to take care of his daughter. At the time, my dad couldn't see that God was using my sister's challenge to catapult him into his ministry. This wasn't a breakdown. This was a buildup for how God was going to use our family to influence thousands of people.

My father was scheduled to preach that night. He told my mom, "I'm going to tell the pastor I can't preach tonight and that I'm going to step back from the ministry." After they arrived at the church, my mom held my sister as Dad made his way to the platform, walking down the center aisle. Halfway down, he felt someone pulling on his coattail. He turned around and was surprised to see a little girl looking up at him. She reached out her hand, and it had a note in it.

She said to my father, "Pastor, God told me to give this to you."

My father patted her on the head, thanked her, and then walked up to the platform to sit down by the head pastor. As he was about to lean over to tell the pastor he couldn't preach and that he was stepping away from the ministry, God spoke to him in his spirit and told him to read the note the little girl had given him. My father reached into his pocket, unfolded the note, and read, "But my God shall supply all of your needs according to His riches in glory in Christ Jesus" (Phil. 4:19).

Something leapt in my dad's spirit. When he read the note, he knew God was with him and his family. Instead of telling the pastor he was stepping back from the ministry, he got up and preached a message about never giving up. Many lives were affected by the message that night, and for the next forty years my dad preached around the world, pastored multiple churches, and influenced thousands of lives.

What happened? When my dad couldn't stand on his own, God gave him a six-year-old giant of the faith on whose shoulders he could stand. Heroes will activate when they are called upon. They are like God's secret agents, sleeper cells that you don't know about until they are activated. That little girl would have been the last person someone would have picked to encourage my parents. But she was what they needed, at just the right time, to keep them going. No matter your age, ethnicity, socioeconomic background, or education—if you're willing to be used when God calls on you, you can become a giant, a hero to someone else.

Several weeks later my mother found out about a world-renowned doctor in San Francisco who had performed rare surgeries for children like my sister. My father and mother met with the doctor at his office but when they found out how much it was going to cost, they knew they could never afford the surgery. The doctor looked at them and said, "Don't worry, we're going to help your baby girl."

With the help of the March of Dimes, my sister's surgery was paid for. My mother took a bus to visit my sister during her recovery, traveling every day back and forth from Porterville while my dad worked. The doctor's wife came in every day to hold my sister and rock her until my mom could get there. A few months after they brought my sister home, she was sitting on the living room floor. To everyone's amazement, she reached for the arm of the couch, pulled herself up, and stood on both legs for the first time. A few days later she took her first steps. She has been walking ever since.

We will never be able to adequately thank the doctor and his wife and the March of Dimes for helping our family in our time of need. We will never be able to thank that little six-year-old girl enough for listening to God and being a hero to my father that day. Instead of looking up at his problems, he stood on her shoulders and looked down at his Goliath. He got a new perspective because of this amazing, tiny giant of the faith.

I've told you that when my wife and I found out about our son Connor's autism, we were devastated. Our world turned upside down in a split second. There were days when it was just too much to handle, and it was difficult as a husband and father to stand on my own. But God will not allow a difficulty to come into our lives unless He has a purpose for it.

We knew we had to find a great school that could help Connor get what he needed. The school we found had amazing behavior specialists who came highly recommended, but it was going to cost forty-two hundred dollars a month. I had just come on staff at Lakewood a year before the diagnosis, and I made a good salary, but that amount of money would take almost everything we had. I told Sam we would do whatever it took to help Connor. We would go down to one car and get an apartment. Whatever it took. I knew this would also affect our other two children, because finances would be too tight to give them things like baseball and dance lessons.

Every night, I heard Sam upstairs crying by Connor's bed after she put him to sleep, saying, "Please, God, make a way to help our son so we don't have to sell our home." She didn't know I was listening, but I could hear every word through the baby monitor in our bedroom. I sat in our bedroom crying as I listened to her. I felt like a failure as a provider because we were going to have to sell our house and my family would have to miss out on so many things. But I knew it was the right thing to do for Connor.

I had told immediate family, but few others, about our situation. It was the week of summer camp at Lakewood, and I was getting ready to head to the church to send our kids and the team off for camp. But first I had to find our realtor's phone number to let him know we needed to sell the house. Oddly enough, I couldn't find the number in time and had to leave for the church without it. While we were heading to the door, I received an unusual phone call from our business administrator. After asking how I was doing, he asked about Connor. This really surprised me, since I had assumed he was calling to discuss something about my budget.

I will never forget what he said next. "Hey, Craig, I just talked to Joel, and we don't want you to have to worry about Connor's schooling or medical bills. We want Connor to have the best schooling and medical help, so Joel wanted me to tell you that it is taken care of." Tears streamed down my cheeks as I thought about my wife sitting next to Connor every night asking God for a miracle. When I called Sam, she wept, saying, "Thank You, Jesus," over and over.

What had just happened? God gave us a giant of the faith with shoulders to stand on. When we couldn't stand on our own, he sent Pastor Joel. From that day forward we had a new vantage point. It was a huge moment in our lives because it gave us the faith and strength to reach out and help others with special needs. Someone became a hero to us so we could become heroes to others.

You have the choice of two lives—the life you're living now and the life within you that could be. If you only stay in the life you're living, you will never find the hidden treasure of the life within you. That's why, even if you're going through a challenge, you can learn to be good to someone else while walking through it. It releases the life within you. Your challenges will teach you strength in a way your victories never could. When you let your faith rise above your circumstances by standing on your heroes' shoulders, and God's, you can elevate others higher than ever before. They'll be standing on your shoulders—the shoulders of a giant.

SEVEN

Live as a Healer

When we think of a healer, we probably think of a doctor, a nurse, a psychologist, or a faith healer. While those are all healers, I believe *everyone* is called to live as a healer. Now, don't run with this and start operating on someone or laying hands on people because I said you're to live as a healer. That may not be your gift—plus you will seriously freak people out if it's not. Living as a healer doesn't make you a doctor, but you can help someone who is hurting with whatever gift you have. Romans 12:8 says, "If your gift is to encourage, be encouraging. If it is giving, give generously. If God has given you leadership ability, take the responsibility seriously. And if you have the gift of showing kindness to others, do it gladly."

Healing comes in different forms. We have no idea what a word of encouragement, a gift out of generosity, or an act of kindness can do for someone else.

Your generosity to someone may be the greatest message you will ever preach. If every person got up every day and decided to perform one act of kindness, I believe a depth of healing would take place that would change mankind profoundly. Why? This is exactly how God operates. I believe God is constantly looking to be good to someone but needs vessels to flow through. It's not that God doesn't want to pour out His goodness; He just doesn't have enough vessels.

As I walked on the journey with Connor, I became a broken vessel. I realized I was not put on this earth to just be a leader; I was put on this earth to be a healer. Many times all you need to do to bring healing to others is to listen or share your story of how you are staying faithful in the middle of adversity. When you can bear someone's pain without breaking, you will give others hope. As Romans 15:1 says, "We who are strong ought to bear the weaknesses of those without strength and not just please ourselves" (NASB).

One Sunday at the beginning of 2014, I made it my mission to live as a healer. I asked God to show me someone I could encourage or help in their time of need. As I was walking through the service during prayer time, I saw a mother crying with her young son who was in a wheelchair. They were praying with one of our prayer partners, and I felt deep down that I was supposed to stop. I waited for the prayer partner to finish praying with them and then took some time to encourage them.

The little boy had a knit cap on his head, and I could tell there was some swelling in the face and around his head area. I thought I remembered someone telling me that he had cancer. The mother said he was scheduled for surgery on the following Tuesday. You could tell she was very concerned. I told her we would have someone visit them at the hospital and someone would call her during her son's surgery. I gave them a hug and then walked back to the front of the sanctuary.

As I was walking away, God spoke to me again and told me to get one of our pastors, John Gray, who was at the front of the church, and walk back with him to where they were sitting and pray with them. The service was in progress, but we had to keep praying. The mother started crying as we knelt to pray for her and her son. It was a beautiful time of prayer, and she thanked us again and again. It wasn't any big deal for us. It was just listening to God and doing the little bit extra to encourage someone else.

Steve, one of our staff members, contacted the mother later and then called me. I asked how the surgery had gone. "It wasn't for cancer," Steve said. "About a year ago the little boy had been following his older brother as he was crossing the street and didn't see a car that was coming from his blind-side. The car hit the little boy as his mother watched." He went on to say that the little boy had had multiple surgeries and a part of his brain removed because of the accident. That day we had prayed with them, he was wearing a knit cap because fluid had built up around the brain. This called for a serious surgery, and his mother wasn't sure he would make it through.

Steve said the mother had been overwhelmed with concern for her son, but when she saw John and me walk all the way from the front to pray for her boy, she said, "I knew God was going to give me a miracle for my son. I knew he would be okay." Sure enough, her son came through the surgery, and they were able to drain the fluid from his brain without complications. As I reflected on this, I thought, *Thank You, God, for letting us live as healers for this wonderful mother and son. We didn't do anything major—just the little extra You asked us to do, and it made such a difference.*

Often we look for big ways to help people, and because they seem so big, we end up doing nothing. I heard someone once say, "In life it's not about the most you can do, it's about the least you can do." Giving half a loaf of bread is better than not giving any bread at all. We should ask ourselves, "What is the least that we can do?" Perhaps it's a smile, a word of encouragement, a prayer, or a small gift. God can take that little and do a lot with it.

One day I received a call from a pastor friend of mine in San Antonio, Pastor Henry, who asked if I would come and help them start a Champions Club for special needs at their church. I said we would be honored to. At the end of the conversation, Pastor Henry asked if I would go with him to visit one of their orphanages in Nuevo Laredo, Mexico, a couple of hours' drive from San Antonio.

I could tell he wanted me to see all the good work they were doing, but I was hesitant because there had been so much violence from drug cartels in the border towns of Texas and Mexico. He assured me it was safe as long as we were with him. I trusted Pastor Henry, but when I checked out what the Department of State website had to say about this part of Mexico, I also saw statements like "extreme caution," "critical threat," and warnings about travel "except for those instances that have been deemed mission essential." I had to pause. When I read those words again, I felt God say in my spirit, *I will protect you. I'm deeming this mission essential.* A peace came over me, so I told Pastor Henry I would go.

We finished some speaking and training at Pastor Henry's church in San Antonio, and then we set out for Nuevo Laredo. As we got closer to the border, we got off the freeway and pulled into a hotel parking lot. Due to the danger, someone from Nuevo Laredo had come to drive us over the border. I saw those words *extreme caution* and *critical threat* scroll across my mind in red flashing letters, and I started praying every prayer I could think of—from dinner prayers and bedtime prayers to "I don't want to die today" prayers. Then I thought, *If we get chased by a drug cartel, and I'm going to die, wouldn't it be cool if we did it Thelma and Louise style? Just hit the gas, and fly off into a canyon. Sure beats being tortured and beheaded like the cartels are doing to people.* These were some of the crazy thoughts crossing my mind at the time. I prayed hard. *Really hard!*

We got to the border and then turned onto back streets to get around the traffic. I kept my eyes on the surroundings, half expecting a van to skid out in front of us and kidnappers to pull out the only gringo in the SUV. Pastor Henry, Pastor Gill, and the driver were speaking in Spanish like it was no big deal. I think they were staying calm to keep me calm. They were probably saying in Spanish, "Look at the crazy gringo about to cry in the back seat."

We kept going down one street and up another. Pastor Henry said to me, "A year ago you couldn't even drive in the early evening like this." He wasn't exactly reassuring me. We finally pulled up to two apartment-style buildings with chipped paint and big gates in front. It looked like there was a courtyard in the middle. I was glad we were there and happy to be alive. As we got out of the car and went up to the gates, I noticed that Pastor Henry seemed so proud. I was excited as well, but I was thinking about how fast we could visit this place and then get across the border before it got completely dark.

Before we knocked on the gate, Pastor Henry turned and told me something I wasn't expecting. When he and his church rehabilitated this orphanage, they brought in children from terrible circumstances. Girls as young as ten years old who had been sex trafficked were living here. There were kids who had been abandoned and abused. The ages ranged from newborn babies to young adults. He said when they first reopened the orphanage, they only had enough money to feed the children once a day on Monday through Saturday. They taught them the principle of fasting on Sundays. It wasn't because they wanted to, but because they didn't have enough food to feed everyone. He said proudly, "But now we feed them three meals a day, seven days a week."

Then Pastor Henry said, "Pastor Craig, when we go in here, don't walk up to the girls until I introduce you." I asked why, and he said that most of them had just come out of sex slavery and they didn't trust men. They trusted him because his ministry had helped them, and he was like a parent to them. But the girls didn't trust strange men. Pastor Henry assured me that when he introduced me, he would explain that I was a good man. At that point, I could reach out and shake their hands. I was shocked by what he had said. I never bargained for an experience like this.

Pastor Henry knocked on the gate, and a young lady opened it slightly, saw who it was, and then opened it wide. She had a broom in her hand and the biggest smile on her face. She called out to Pastor Henry, calling him "Papa," and then hugs ensued as if it were a family reunion. Pastor Henry and his wife have been like parents to many of these orphans. The one who opened the door was a young adult about nineteen years old. One of her chores was to sweep and clean the courtyard every day. You would have thought by the look on her face that it was the greatest job on the planet. After she greeted Pastor Henry and Gill, she saw me and then stepped back. Her smile went away. I asked Pastor Henry why she was so afraid. He told me how, from an early age, this young girl was sold by her parents to any man who would pay them.

"She has had every imaginable thing happen to her," he said. "One night she was lying in her bed, and she had a vision that she ran away from her house, walked up to a big gate and knocked on the door. When a person opened the door, she saw a huge courtyard filled with happy children playing in it. She didn't know where this place was or if it even existed, but this vision gave her the courage to decide to run away.

"So one day she sneaked out of her house and ran away with no money or food. She wandered the streets for a few days until she saw a gate like the one in her dream. She walked up to the gate, tired and weak from hunger. When someone opened the door, she saw the courtyard with children playing inside, and it was the exact same picture she had seen in her vision. Standing there amazed, she knew then that God had given her the vision and brought her to safety. The orphanage welcomed her with open arms, and she's been there ever since. The reason she is happy sweeping is because she is so grateful to be here in this crowded orphanage where there is so much love, instead of being in her parents' home where there was so much evil. This place is like heaven for her. That's why she smiles all the time."

Pastor Henry then looked at her with a gentle smile and said in Spanish, *"Mija,* this is Pastor Craig. He's a good man." When he said this, her smile came back, and she reached out and even gave me a hug. It was a beautiful moment.

As we walked in, children of all ages saw Pastor Henry and Gill and mobbed them like they were movie stars. Pastor Henry high-fived and hugged them one by one. He tried to make everyone feel important. Then he came upon a little girl about ten years old. She had been sold into prostitution when she was only eight. Just like the other girl, she gave Pastor Henry a big hug, but when she saw me, she pulled back away from the strange man in front of her. Pastor Henry said, *"Mija,* this is Pastor Craig. He's a good man." Then this precious little ten-year-old girl reached out and gave me a smile and a hug. This happened time and time again. It was one girl after another with the same story of despair, now finding hope.

Then we came to the babies. The first little boy we met in his crib was named Daniel. That wasn't his real name. They didn't know his real name. He had no papers because his mom knew she couldn't feed him and had delivered him just thirty minutes before she showed up at the front gates of the orphanage. She had the baby in one hand and the placenta and umbilical cord in a bag still connected to the baby in the other. The mother was crying, and all she could do was hand them the baby and the bag. The orphanage workers took him in, and he's been there ever since, being cared for by the teens and young adults.

In the next crib was a lovely little girl with rosy cheeks, big brown eyes, and the most beautiful brown hair you've ever seen. I asked if I could hold her and was told it was okay. At first she moved her head back away from me, but she slowly nuzzled closer as I rocked her back and forth. Eventually she became comfortable enough to put her cheek next to mine, staying there for at least ten minutes. Pastor Henry said we probably needed to go, so I began to put her back in her crib. As I went to put her down, she began to reach up for me with both hands, crying for me to hold her again. I asked Pastor Henry what I should do. He said, "You had better pick her up. She really likes you." I picked her up, and as I brought her close to me, she put her arms around me, hugged me tightly, and would not let me go.

I asked Pastor Henry about this baby girl's story. He said

she was found on the streets of Nuevo Laredo, wandering around in a diaper. Her mother had apparently dropped her off in the middle of the street and never returned. She had no name, no record of even being born. Right then I heard God speak to me and say, *You wanted to reach the forgotten. Now you are.*

I had told God I wanted to reach those with special needs, those who were forgotten and overlooked by society. But that day God showed me that I was to live as a healer, not only to those with special needs but also to those who had no name. He said in my spirit, *Everywhere you go there are people in need, forgotten by society and even their own families. I want you to teach people to reach out to others, live as healers, restoring the brokenhearted and bringing healing wherever they go.*

That day I named the little girl Cara. It is of Latin, Irish, and Gaelic origin, and it means "beloved friend." She is not forgotten anymore. Now she is a friend of God, His beloved. As I reluctantly left the nursery, both Cara and I were crying. I wanted to take her home with me, but I knew that without any papers it would be difficult for her to be adopted. We are still praying that someday someone—whether it is us or another beautiful family—will adopt Cara, the beloved friend.

Pastor Henry then took me down a long hallway of the courtyard and said, "Pastor Craig, I want to tell you the main reason I brought you here today." He stopped walking and pointed to a girl sitting on the other side of the courtyard in a makeshift wheelchair being pushed by one of the young adults. I could tell she had severe cerebral palsy, the kind that twists the face, arms, and legs. He told me a story I will never forget.

"The girl in the wheelchair is named Gladys," he said. "That's not her real name. We do not know her real name. She has no papers, but we think she is now sixteen years old. Two years ago I received a call to come as quickly as I could to a place near the banks of the river here in Nuevo Laredo. We found that this girl with severe cerebral palsy had been stripped naked, gang raped, and thrown out of a van on the banks of the river to die.

"When someone found her, they called the orphanage and then called my wife and me to come and help. I couldn't believe what I was hearing on the phone. How could someone do this to a fourteen-year-old handicapped girl? We quickly drove down to where she was, and there she was lying on the bank of the river, naked and shaking. My wife and I got out of our car with a blanket and covered her abused little body, and I looked at her and said, 'No one will ever hurt you again, *mija*. I am taking you to a safe place where no one will ever hurt you again.'"

As he told this story to me, we walked closer to Gladys, and Pastor Henry said, "We brought her here, Pastor Craig, and we have loved and cared for her. Now she is not as traumatized as she once was." Right about then, Gladys saw us coming toward her. As she saw Pastor Henry, she reached out her elbows—because her arms wouldn't bend—and cried out, "Papa, Papa, Papa!" Pastor Henry reached down, embraced her, and said, "*Mija*, it's so good to see you. You look so beautiful today." They hugged and exchanged smiles. She then saw me and, like the other girls, pulled back, wondering who I was. Pastor Henry said, *"Mija,* this is Pastor Craig; he's a good man." Immediately, she reached out her elbows and, with a big contorted smile, gave me the most beautiful hug I've ever received.

Then Pastor Henry pointed and said, "Pastor Craig, the main reason I brought you here today is that I want to ask you a favor. Do you see that section of the orphanage?"

I nodded, tears still rolling down my face from the emotional moment with Gladys.

"We want that to be the new Champions Club developmental center for special needs here at the orphanage," he explained. "We can take care of Gladys, but we can't develop her so she can be everything God has purposed her to be. But you can. We're going to help Gladys and other kids who are severely disabled and thrown out of their houses like garbage to die. We are going to bring them to the Champions Club and help them be everything God wants them to be."

When you have an opportunity to make a difference in other people's lives, learn to follow that love. Act on it. If I had not listened to God and had been afraid to go to Mexico, I would have missed out on being a blessing to those who needed it most.

That trip wasn't just about bringing healing to Gladys; it was as much about bringing healing to me. When you position yourself to live as a healer, God will also bring healing to you. I can't tell you how washed by love I was that day. The generosity in that orphanage was like a healing rain to my soul. I would never be the same again.

EIGHT

Victim or Victor

It's easy to fall into the victim mentality. Let's face it, when you're a casualty or injured party, it can take the life right out of you. When you are down, the Enemy wants to keep you down. If you've ever watched professional wrestlers put on a show, they love to knock their opponent down and keep them down until they lose the match. They will throw a fake kick, a fake elbow, a fake punch to the jaw, one right after another.

One of my favorites is the sleeper hold, when one of the wrestlers takes one arm and places it across the top of their opponent's head and then places the other arm underneath their chin. As he holds on and applies more pressure, the other wrestler begins to fall into a "deep sleep."

When I was a kid, I thought that was fantastic, so I once tried it with one of my neighborhood friends. Let's just say it didn't go well. He started yelling that I was choking him, and I kept yelling, "You're getting sleepier, sleepier, sleepier!" He didn't sleep and went home crying to his mom. I got in trouble. Honestly, I wasn't upset that I got in trouble. I was upset that I did the sleeper hold exactly as I had seen it done, and it didn't work.

But there is nothing fake about getting punched in the stomach by life. It can sometimes feel like one kick, elbow, and punch after another. Except the Enemy doesn't just want you down; he wants you out. Since God won't let him take you out, the Enemy's goal might be to put you to sleep. He wants us so dazed by life that we walk around in a catatonic state, a mental stupor. This is the Enemy's "sleeper hold." If we let him keep us in this hold, soon we become victims of our circumstances. We are alive on the outside but near death on the inside.

In the weeks after we first got Connor's diagnosis and began to hear from the doctors that there was no cure for autism, I remember being in a fog. I was still going to work, still walking through life, but I was in a dazed and confused state. Then I began to experience fear and anger. I didn't know what to do, and the problem wasn't going anywhere. As a matter of fact, when Connor was only three years old, experts were telling us what our son was going to be and what our life was going to be like. I could feel the victim mentality rearing its ugly head.

When you're going through something that hurts, it's natural to want sympathy. Healing is a process, and healing will come if you keep the right perspective—even when the problems continue. For us, autism and its challenges did not go away. What we had to decide was how we would let it affect us and how we were going to respond to it. Our flesh wanted to respond negatively. Our faith wanted to respond positively. It was a war between the mentality of a victim and that of a victor.

This is a crossroads moment. It's a lot easier to get into the victim mentality than it is to get out. The challenge is that being a victim won't just hurt the brokenhearted; it will affect everyone he or she loves and cares for. Victims spread the disease when deep down that is not their intention. They just want the pain to stop.

You can always identify victims. They are the ones pointing to their scars. They remind themselves of what has happened and struggle to see the purpose of the journey they are on. Except for some glimpses of happiness, they mostly focus on the pain. Some "victims," with other complications such as mental illness, might require counseling and medical guidance to help them walk on their journeys. They may not be able to fully comprehend how to separate the victim and victor mentalities. Most of us can make that distinction. We do have a choice, no matter how difficult the situation may be.

"Well," someone might say, "you don't know what I've been through. You can never understand when you haven't walked a mile in my shoes." My intention is not to minimize what anyone has gone through. The truth is that all of us have walked a mile in different shoes, and no matter how rocky our hill was, there is always someone who has walked through something worse.

I would never want to make light of the hurt and pain someone has gone through any more than I would like it to happen to me. Yet if you put two people together, and both have been through the same painful situation—one choosing to embrace the pain, and the other choosing to embrace the purpose—there is usually a different outcome. When you embrace the pain, only one thing can return: more pain. When you embrace the purpose God is trying to accomplish, your heart will begin to open to see the possibilities.

There were once two beautiful families that lived in the same town. The Richardsons had three children, Chris, Trae, and Nicole—two boys and a girl. The Hayes family had one girl because they could not conceive any more children after they had their daughter. Her name was Sophie. They were both very close-knit families.

Nicole Richardson and Sophie Hayes were best friends and were inseparable. When they were teenagers, one night after a basketball game, they were driving in Sophie's car to meet some friends at a burger joint. They were crossing an intersection when a car coming from the other direction ran a red light and T-boned Sophie's car, killing her instantly and throwing Nicole out of the car onto the street. Nicole's body was broken and mangled, but she was still alive. An ambulance rushed her to the hospital where she almost died. They resuscitated Nicole, but shortly after she came out of surgery, she went into a coma.

The police contacted the girls' parents. Nicole's parents

rushed to her side in the ICU. The Hayeses, weeping, drove to the accident site to meet with police and were told their daughter Sophie had passed away. As they looked in horror, in the seat of her yellow Volkswagen bug, they saw a white sheet draped over their only child's lifeless body.

Mrs. Hayes fell to her knees as Mr. Hayes tried to hold her up; they were hanging on to each other in disbelief.

Sitting on the curb were two boys who attended the same school as Nicole and Sophie and who had just returned from a party. They had some beers that night before getting in their car. As they drove, they were talking about a girl one of them liked who was at the party. When the driver turned his head to look at the passenger, he ran through the stoplight into the intersection. They broadsided the girls' car, and in an instant everyone's life changed. Besides a few scratches and bruises, the boys were fine.

Sophie's father looked away from his daughter's body and looked over at the two boys who had their heads bowed, sitting on the edge of the curb. The driver of the car lifted his head, and his tear-filled eyes met Sophie's father's eyes. The first thought that came to the father's mind was how young everyone was who had been involved. The second thought was how something so senseless could have taken his baby girl from him.

At the hospital the Richardsons sat by Nicole's side as the respirator pumped air into her lungs. The doctor came in and said, "Mr. and Mrs. Richardson, I know how difficult this must be for you both."

Mr. Richardson snapped back, "Has this ever happened to your daughter?"

The doctor shook his head.

"Then you have no idea how difficult this is for us! Look at her!"

The doctor leaned in and said, "Mr. and Mrs. Richardson, there is no easy way for me to say this, but your daughter's brain is not functioning."

Mrs. Richardson looked up and said, "You mean she is brain dead?"

The doctor responded, "There is no brain function. It looks like when she was thrown from the car, she severely hit her head on the pavement. I'm very sorry."

The Richardsons embraced each other, and then suddenly Mr. Richardson let out a scream, "Why? Why? Who did this to my girl?"

The next day, in anguish and pain, the Richardsons decided to let Nicole go. As they watched her take her last breath after the removal of the ventilator, Mr. Richardson only felt hurt and anger. He left the hospital, drove to the police station, and demanded to speak to the officer on duty. When an officer came to talk to him, he said, "I want that boy who was driving that car to pay! I want him charged with murder!"

The officer assured Mr. Richardson there would be due process and encouraged him to let the authorities take care of the situation. As Mr. Richardson left the station, he kept yelling, "I want him to pay for what he did!"

Mr. and Mrs. Hayes were hurting terribly as well. They had so many emotions swirling around them. One minute they felt anger; the next minute they felt sadness. They had lost their only child. During the next few days, each family planned their daughter's funeral. During that time the families coped the best they could.

Emotions were running high and low, depending on the moment. The parents of the boy who was driving the car were devastated. Their son was arrested and arraigned for manslaughter. If convicted, he could face a minimum of two and a maximum of twenty years in prison. The authorities released him on bail, and all he did was sit in his room, replaying in his mind what had happened. He sobbed, regained his composure, and then sobbed again. The other boy in the car, the passenger, was released.

The driver's parents reached out and called the Richardsons, who were too upset to speak with them. The boy's parents said they understood and then dialed the number of the Hayeses. A family member picked up the phone. At first Mr. and Mrs. Hayes didn't want to take the call. But then Mrs. Hayes looked at her husband and said, "Not many parents whose son just made this kind of mistake would have the courage to call the families of the victims."

Mr. Hayes nodded his head and went to the phone. "Hello?" he said. "This is Mr. Hayes."

For the next few minutes the boy's parents cried and apologized for what had happened. They said they knew they couldn't ease the pain the Hayeses were going through, but they wanted them to know how truly sorry they were for the mistake their son had made. They hoped that someday the Hayeses would be able to forgive him. Mr. Hayes struggled to speak, but, at the end of the call, thanked them for calling and told them good night.

The families decided that, because the girls were best friends, they would have separate funerals but a joint memorial service at the high school the girls had attended. Hundreds of students, faculty, family, and friends came to the memorial service. Even the parents of the boy who was driving the car came. They were good people who loved their son and knew he had made a terrible mistake. They knew they could do nothing to take back what their son had done, but they did not want to hide in shame and not convey how sorry they were for what had happened.

Some were shocked to see them there. Whispers went across the room as they walked in and sat down. Because the boys who were driving the car were well liked before the incident, the room was split. Some were disgusted, but others knew how hard it must have been for the boy's parents to come, and so they looked on them with tentative grace.

When the memorial service was over, members of the crowd stood in line to hug and comfort the girls' families. At the end of the line, the parents of the boy who had run the red light, with bowed heads, slowly approached first the Richardsons. When Mr. Richardson saw them, all his pain and anger rose inside of him, and as they came close, he put his arm around his wife and walked away.

The boy's mother broke down crying, and the father put his arm around her and slowly walked to the next aisle where Sophie's parents stood. They had seen what had happened. They fully understood why the Richardsons felt the way they did. Yet, instead of letting the pain and anger overtake them, they felt compassion for the boy's parents. They weren't sure why, because deep in their hearts they were feeling the same pain as the Richardsons, and they knew they were looking at the parents of the boy whose drunk driving had ended their only daughter's life.

As the boy's parents walked up, the Hayeses, with their heads bowed and crying, reached out their arms, embraced the boy's parents, and began to console them, saying, "It took a lot of courage for you to come today. Most people in your situation could not have done what you did under the circumstances. Thank you for honoring our daughter by being here today."

Then Mr. Hayes reached out and whispered in the boy's parents' ears, "Tell your son we forgive him."

The boy's parents were so overwhelmed by the grace that had just been bestowed upon them that all they could say again and again was, "Thank you. We're so sorry. Thank you."

As the boy's parents walked away, one of the family members asked Mr. and Mrs. Hayes how they could forgive someone who had taken their most precious daughter from them. Mrs. Hayes said, with tears in her eyes, "It's hard enough to live with the hurt of losing your child and at the same time carry the pain of unforgiveness. I could not live with that, and neither could they."

During the next few years, though the Richardsons and Hayeses experienced the same tragedy, they lived two very different lives. The Richardsons reminded themselves every day of their scars. They rarely thought about the good memories because they couldn't get past the pain. When the boy was sentenced to three years in prison, Mr. Richardson's pain and anger went to another level.

"That is not enough!" he told the boy's parents as he walked out of the courtroom.

From prison, the boy wrote each family a letter saying how sorry he was for making a terrible mistake and bringing so much pain to their families. He asked if they could find it in their hearts to forgive him someday. Mr. and Mrs. Richardson would not even read the letter. After someone read the letter to them, they offered no response and threw the letter away.

In the next few years their home changed from being full of life and love to a place no one in the family would have recognized. Mr. and Mrs. Richardson stayed together but were never the same. They closed themselves off from friends and family. Their own two boys, after leaving for college, could not stand going back home because of the cloud that hung over their mom and dad. They could never get past the pain. They became victims of their circumstances.

The Hayeses' lives played out a little differently. The first couple of years were hard, but slowly, as the days went by, the pain got a little easier. Not having their daughter around made the house quiet, so they became youth leaders at their church and hosted a small group every other Friday night.

They started a grief-share program at their church where others who had been through similar situations of loss could share their stories and encourage each other as they walked through them together.

The boy spent the first month of his sentence in the juvenile detention center, and Mr. Hayes asked the boy's father if he could visit him. As Mr. Hayes arrived, the boy stood to his feet, unsure what Mr. Hayes would say. Mr. Hayes then reached out his arms, gave him a hug and said, "I forgave you when I saw you sitting on the curb. I knew that if I didn't, my daughter wouldn't have been the only one who died that day. I would have died with her. Now I want you to live the rest of your life like she would have lived hers—with love, purpose, and grace."

The boy looked at Mr. Hayes and said, "Yes sir, I will, I will. I won't let you down again."

Mr. Hayes smiled and said, "It's not me you would let down; it's Sophie. Don't let her down. Live for her. Can you do that?"

With tears rolling down his cheeks because of the grace he had just received, the boy firmly nodded. Without fail Mr. Hayes visited the boy every week until he was released. Because of Mr. and Mrs. Hayeses' grace and forgiveness, they could live the rest of their lives not as victims but as victors. So could the boy who was driving the car. To the Hayeses, he's not the boy who drove the car that killed their daughter; he's now the boy saved by grace whose name is Kevin.

Two families experienced the same tragedy, yet one chose

the victim mentality, and the other chose the victor mentality. Honestly, I'm not judging either choice. The pain of losing a child is almost incomprehensible. It would be easy to be victimized by such a circumstance. But even if you've lost something so great, you are still alive. There is reason for our pain. As John Gray says, "You don't get sentenced with pain, you get trusted with it."

The Bible contains many stories illustrating that we never should bow to the Enemy, no matter the pain of our circumstances. For example, after much suffering, Joseph told his brothers, "You intended to harm me, but God intended it all for good. He brought me to this position so I could save the lives of many people" (Gen. 50:20).

You were brought to this pain in your life to be a testimony for those who need to relate to someone who's been there, done that, and is still standing. In challenging times we discover who is willing to fight despite the odds. Heroes of the faith become heroes during challenging times.

When the Enemy tries to give you the *victim* label, tear it off, get a marker, and make one that says, *"Victor."* You were put on this earth to overcome every label the Enemy has tried to put on you. Tear off the tags of *failure, loser, unworthy*. Put on the tags of *successful, winner, invaluable*. You are a warrior for the King. You cannot be defeated. Wear your new labels proudly.

When you do, get ready: You are about to change the world! You are moving from victim to victor!

NINE

Out of the Drought

believe today could be unlike any other day in your life. You may say, "Craig, what makes this day special? It seems pretty normal to me." But today, what if you took one outrageous step of faith that could change problems you've been dealing with for years? Would you do it? It might look crazy to others. But sometimes in life you need to forget your dignity and put your faith out there.

Let me give you some out-of-the-ordinary examples of becoming undignified to reach a breakthrough. You may have seen the first one if you've been to New York City. His name is Robert John Burck, but he's better known as the Naked Cowboy. He is a street performer who wears nothing but a cowboy hat, boots, and boxer briefs and walks out in the middle of Times Square asking for money. The funny thing is that people give him the money—around $150,000 a year! He even has an endorsement with Fruit of the Loom, a company that makes his underwear. I think he also ran for president in 2012 but, surprisingly, fell short.

Another guy named Nicholas wanted to get a job so badly he did something out of the norm. Instead of turning in a paper resume, he turned in a chocolate resume. That's right, a resume made from a chocolate bar, with the tagline on the wrapper, "Credentials that would satisfy any organization's appetite." His delicious chocolate resume got him the job. I guess it's true that everyone likes chocolate.[1]

Speaking of people who love food . . . I once did something crazy and drove four hundred miles round trip just to eat at a hole-in-the-wall restaurant that claimed to have the best tacos in California. Nuts, right? It turned out they were as good as advertised. It was a taco epiphany. The best I had ever eaten. To me it was even worth the heartburn and gas I had all the way home after downing a personal record of eighteen tacos in two hours. It hurt so good.

John Osteen used to ask, "How big is your 'want to'?" I would also ask, how undignified are you willing to get to reach your breakthrough? How boldly will you pray? How far will you go? Because I promise you—God has planned something good for you on the other side of your drought, your time of dryness and waiting.

In the last four years, my wife and I have experienced some of the most amazingly blessed times in our lives, after coming through some of the longest droughts. When you're in the middle of a drought, though, breakthrough seems far away.

The doors don't even get slammed in your face anymore; they stay locked and closed. Have you ever found yourself in a place like that, where nothing is happening but the problems keep coming? It is, as the psalmist put it, like walking in the valley of the shadow of death.

When you have a child with autism, and doctors tell you there is no cure except working through it, that doesn't exactly give you a lot of hope. It's like someone saying, "This is your lot in life. Deal with it." You have probably been told at some point that if you make wrong choices, something bad will happen to you and you will be cursed for that choice for the rest of your life. This view sees God as vindictive and too righteous to accept us, especially when we make mistakes. So not only are we dealing with the challenge, but we are also carrying a truckload of guilt that gets dumped on us whenever we're reminded of something we've done wrong.

If you have been taught this, I want to clear something up before we go any further. This is not the God I know. Yes, we all face consequences for mistakes we make. That is life. But it doesn't mean God caused them, and it doesn't mean this is your lot in life. God is a God of grace who wants to help us, not hurt us. Even if you make wrong decisions, your life is not over.

God is not furious with you. His love is chasing you down. Would someone madly in love with you want to curse you and keep you in a dry place for the rest of your life? Of course not. They would do the opposite. Max Lucado said, "How much does God love us? God would give up His only son before He would give up on you."[2] So lay down the notion that because you are sick, because your marriage is struggling, because you have a child with special needs, that this is your lot in life and you are cursed. Refreshing waters are on the other side of that drought.

When the soldiers looked up at Jesus on the cross, they had to be thinking, *What a sad conclusion. This guy's life is over.* But the truth of the matter was, His sacrifice gave us a chance for new life. God was looking at the perfect sacrifice to save the world. In the same way you aren't down and out in God's eyes. You are a beautifully perfect testimony waiting to happen, because He sees Jesus in you.

Some of you have been going through seasons of drought so long that you've forgotten what rain feels like. Whether your drought has been six months or six years, I believe something is about to change. I want you to get ready for a breakthrough. You're coming out of the drought and into the abundance of rain.

Scripture encourages us:

> What joy for those whose strength comes from
> the Lord,
> who have set their minds on a pilgrimage to
> Jerusalem.
> When they walk through the Valley of Weeping,
> it will become a place of refreshing springs.
> The autumn rains will clothe it with blessings.
> They will continue to grow stronger,

and each of them will appear before God in
Jerusalem.
(Ps. 84:5–8)

When you believe, you are not only going to make it through this drought, but you are going to build a reservoir of faith for the droughts to come. Once you've conquered your desert, you won't respond to the next desert the same way. You move from rookie to veteran, from beginner to pro, from survivor to overcomer. Your tests, as they say, become your testimonies!

In these times, pray bold prayers—not "just get by" prayers, but bold prayers! Maybe even undignified prayers—the kind that may seem crazy to those outside looking in. Psalm 34 says, "I prayed to the LORD, and He answered me." Psalm 22 says, "They cried out to you and were saved. In you they trusted and were not disappointed." During a drought, we have the option to complain and grumble instead of praying bold prayers. But there is no power in complaining. I've heard it said that disappointments are inevitable, but misery is optional.

In the Old Testament, when God was bringing the children of Israel out of Egypt and into the promised land flowing with milk and honey, the trip was only supposed to take eleven days. The children of Israel began to complain and murmur, and a journey that should have taken less than two weeks ended up lasting forty years. Complaining is the language of the disempowered; the One with all the power doesn't speak that language. God is moved by our faith, not our complaints.

I know that when we initially face hard things, we might need to release feelings so we can get them off our chest. But let me encourage you not to stay in the land of murmuring. As the children of Israel learned, it will take you nowhere. Instead, pray bold prayers.

My wife and I found out how effective bold prayers can be when we were going through a drought with Connor. We were overwhelmed at times. Many children with autism struggle with the task of going to the restroom on their own. You'll remember that for years we tried every method you can think of to potty train Connor. He was now seven years old, and he had moved from kids' diapers to adult diapers because he was getting so big. We never stopped trying. We constantly experimented with different methods and only used diapers when we didn't have any other choice. When we were potty training at home, it seemed like we had to watch him 24/7.

Many times he had accidents when we were in a public place like a restaurant or swimming pool (including that memorable pool incident we talked about in chapter 3). We were so mortified and desperate for things to change that we would have tried just about anything. It was going on a five-year drought, and we desperately wanted it to end. We wanted our son to reach this milestone as a testament to his ability to overcome obstacles in his life. Those milestones were few and far between, so we celebrated each one.

During this time I happened to be in Washington, DC, for an event called the Night of Hope at the Nationals' Stadium. There I had the chance to meet with Mark Batterson. Mark was pastoring National Community Church, sometimes called the "theater church" because many of their locations are theaters. They are doing an amazing work in the nation's capital. Mark also has written successful inspirational books.

The day we met, our conversation swung toward our families, and I shared with him about what Connor was going through with his potty training. He was moved by the story and said, "You know, I am about to release a new book called *The Circle Maker*, which is about praying bold prayers. Let me send you a copy. I think it will help."

I thanked him, and we went our separate ways. On the plane ride home, I could hear God saying, *You need to read this book when it comes. This is for you.* So when I received it in the mail, I jumped right into it. In the first part, Mark talks about a story of a man named Honi who dared to pray bold prayers and became a legend to his people:

> It was the first century BC, and a devastating drought threatened to destroy a generation . . . But there was one man, an eccentric sage who lived outside the walls of Jerusalem, who dared to pray anyway. His name was Honi. And even if the people could no longer hear God, he believed that God could still hear them. . . .
>
> When rain is plentiful, it's an afterthought. During a drought, it's the only thought.[3]

How true that statement is. If you've ever been in a weather-related drought, the only thing most people are talking about is the drought. It's true when we're going through a life drought as well. Do you notice it's the only thing on your mind most of the time? Just to get a break from thinking about it is a relief.

The story continues:

> With a six-foot staff in his hand, Honi began to turn like a math compass. . . . Honi stood inside the circle he had drawn. Then he dropped to his knees and raised his hands to heaven. . . . Honi called down rain:
>
> *"Lord of the universe, I swear before Your great name that I will not move from this circle until You have shown mercy upon Your children."*
>
> Then it happened. . . .
>
> Raindrops descended to the earth. . . . The people rejoiced over each drop, but Honi wasn't satisfied with a sprinkle. Still kneeling within the circle, Honi lifted his voice over the sounds of celebration:
>
> "Not for such rain have I prayed, but for rain that will fill cisterns, pits, and caverns."[4]

Honi knew that God was bigger than just some rain. Honi served a big God. He didn't just want rain. He was believing for a flood. Some of us would settle for a little rain. But if we asked, God would give us a flood of His blessings.

It rained so heavily and so steadily that the people fled to the Temple Mount to escape the flash floods. Honi stayed and prayed inside his protracted circle. Once more he refined his bold request:

"Not for such rain have I prayed, but for rain of Your favor, blessing, and graciousness."

. . . It began to rain calmly, peacefully. Each raindrop was a token of God's grace."[5]

I thought to myself, *Why can't God do something like that for us?* Of course, I didn't have a staff like Honi did, lying around the house, but I did have a green Swiffer. Sam and I took that Swiffer, and we began to draw our circle. We weren't going to draw a small circle, either. We serve a big God, and we would draw big circles. We walked around Connor's bedroom, we walked around our car, we started walking around our house with the green Swiffer, praying bold prayers. I think our neighbors were probably looking at us like we were two cards short of a full deck.

But we didn't care. How big was our "want to"? Our "want to" was huge. We had had enough of this seven-year drought with our son. We were coming out of the drought and into the abundance of rain, and if it came with someone labeling us with the "crazy" tag, it was well worth it. Sometimes you have to get a little crazy. Sometimes you have to be a little undignified.

As we drew our circle, we made bold declarations like, "God, we have waited for our son to be potty trained long enough. We've tried everything we know to do. Now, do what You do best. You said to come boldly to the throne of grace, and there we will find grace to help us when we need it most! God, we need it most now! We know You have the power to do it for us."

For two weeks we drew our circles and made these prayer declarations.

Then it happened.

On a Saturday afternoon Connor, who in almost seven years of life had not gone to the bathroom by himself, was playing in the backyard. He suddenly stopped playing and opened the back door, walked past us in the living room, walked into the bathroom, and went to the potty all by himself for the first time. It was a miracle! We were in shock.

We ran into the bathroom and yelled, "Connor, are you going to the potty by yourself?" He just looked at us like it was no big deal. We danced around the house. The rain was falling, and it wasn't just a drizzle, it was a flood of God's goodness. Connor has been going to the bathroom by himself ever since.

How big is your "want to"? Are you willing to get a little undignified to come out of your situation? If God can do it for us, can't He do it for you? Get your Swiffer, broom, hockey stick, or whatever you can find to draw your circle. Don't draw a small circle. Draw the biggest one you can because He is a big God. Begin to pray bold prayers. Watch what God will do.

You may be in a drought today. You may have forgotten what rain feels like. Let me encourage you: This is your time; your drought is over. Just like they call Honi's story the "Legend of the Circle Maker," I believe new legends are going to be born. Your children, grandchildren, and great-grandchildren are going to be talking about your testimony of God's goodness.

I declare over you that you are coming out of the drought and into the abundance of rain. What God is bringing you through at this very moment is going to become the testimony that will bring somebody else through their drought. No mess, no message. Your life just became the message. You have been picked to be a messenger of hope. You're coming out of the drought and into the abundance of rain.

TEN

Not-So-Ordinary Miracles

A child playing with friends, a little girl having a conversation with her mother, a middle school boy going to the bathroom by himself, a father and son playing catch—to some these scenes may seem very ordinary. But to others they would be miracles. It's amazing what the human mind is conditioned to believe is ordinary and what is a miracle.

Our son Connor spoke to us from the time he was one and saying his first word to the time he was a two-year-old chatterbox. This was somewhat normal to us. Our other two children, Cory and Courtney, who are ten and twelve years older than Connor, were the same way. They talked incessantly. We thought every child did this.

My son Cory, at a very young age, loved to watch a video about David and Goliath called *Super Book*. He would walk around with a plastic sword and cloth sling and proclaim as he swung his sling, "I will slay you, Gowiath [Goliath], in the name of the Lo-ward [Lord]. For Him is on my side!" The imaginary stone would be thrown, and he would then run over and knock down a toy Transformer, pull his sword out, and with a mighty swing cut off the Transformer's head, which we had to tape back on over and over. He would then proclaim, as he held the Transformer's head in his hand, "God has dewivered this Phiwistine into my hand!" I don't know how biblically correct it was, but it was hilarious watching him do this. This is normal, right? Every kid does this.

Fast-forward to when my Connor was two years old. We would often hear him say without hesitation, "I love you." Then, without much warning, he said nothing. Where previously he had played with other kids, he would sit in a corner and only play by himself. What at one time seemed ordinary now would be a miracle. For the next three years, we would barely hear our son put two words together.

We take so much for granted in life because it seems to happen naturally. I remember finding this out firsthand the first time I experienced a hurricane after coming to Houston. When the hundred-mile-an-hour winds and rain finally stopped, there was no electricity and no running water for days. What had seemed so ordinary a few days before became scarce and precious in an instant.

The truth is that life is a miracle. Miracles happen around us every day. Life depends on the little things we take for granted. One might imagine the most important of life's miracles are big. But it's God at work in the little things that shows how big God is. They are clever illusions to the human eye, but if you looked through God's magnifying glass, they would be supernatural phenomena that make life happen every day.

No one understands that more than a special-needs parent. When you were preparing with joy and excitement to have your new baby, you dreamed about all the things your child was going to do. But it didn't turn out that way. God had a scarier, bigger plan. You thought your child would do ordinary things like others, but God was going to show you miracles no one else could see, a blind spot coming into full view.

For instance, in America anyone can ask for and get a drink of clean or bottled water. Seems ordinary, right? Yet it would be a not-so-ordinary miracle for a child in Africa who lives in a community where the only water they have access to is dirty and diseased. A little girl having a conversation with her mommy seems ordinary for many parents, don't you think? But, for my wife, Sam, and me to hear one sentence from our son after years of silence would have been beyond a miracle. Having a healthy child—outside of a cold or flu— would seem ordinary for most parents, right? Yet, to my friend Barb Dittrich, who has seen her children in and out of hospitals for years, this would be an amazing miracle. Barb shares her story from her own perspective:

Back when genetic testing was imperfect, we were informed that the results we got were inconclusive and there may be a chance that we could be the parents of a child with hemophilia. *Hemophilia* refers to a group of inherited disorders that cause abnormal bleeding. . . . Symptoms of hemophilia range from increased bleeding after trauma, injury, or surgery to sudden bleeding with no apparent cause.

We went about thinking, *Not us! We've been through enough trials already.* You see, our children had not come easily to us, and going through miscarriages and extensive fertility treatment, we had also faced other hurdles in our lives. Foolishly, we believed we had reached our "trauma quotient" for the next twenty years!

The shock of our son's diagnosis hit us like a ton of bricks the day after he was born. "There is no easy way to say this. He has hemophilia," the doctor declared upon entering my hospital room. Having had two nephews with the disorder, we had a vague idea of the expense and struggle we all faced in our future. Nevertheless, through tears and disbelief we whispered in prayer together, "Thank You, God, for hemophilia. We're not sure why we're thanking You, but we thank You anyway."[1]

Why was she thanking God for the hemophilia? In the days ahead she would struggle with countless visits to the hospital, financial burdens, and numerous other challenges. So how could she find the miracle in the tragedy? Barbara said it like this: "Thank You, God, for hemophilia because, in our struggles, others may find hope."[2] She saw the miracle God was using her to bring hope, like very few could, because He knew she could carry hope while He carried her struggles. You can't see all the miracles God is doing if your thoughts are entrenched in your own situational pain. I can't tell you how much power there is behind the principle of seeing the miracle in the pain. Can you see what God sees, even when surrounded by negativity?

I believe we need to celebrate what we do have, not what we don't have. Look at what's right in your life, not what's wrong. Instead of Barb seeing the hemophilia, she saw the miracle that first, she had a son. After going through miscarriages and extensive fertility treatments, it was a miracle that she and her husband could have a child at all.

One of my good friends, Javier, had a nephew with autism who didn't speak. He would have severe seizures, and the hard part for his parents was that he could never express his feelings through words. Their son tragically died while having a seizure when taking a bath. When I asked Mr. and Mrs. Solis, the parents, how they were doing, they said something very powerful to me: "With all our son's challenges, we know many people would find this to be a relief, but for us, we loved our son so much, and he was such a huge part of our lives—as a matter of fact, he was our life. We miss him so much, and we would give anything to have him back with us now."

It's hard to imagine facing the challenges of taking care of a child twenty-four hours a day. Yet these parents saw what many struggle to see—the things that were right with their son—which made the pain of his challenges not only bearable, but inspirational. Their love was unconditional. That's the deepest form of love one can ever experience. That is love that only God truly understands. When you experience unconditional love like that, you are experiencing heaven on earth.

We have so much to be grateful for, despite our challenges. There is always someone in a more challenging situation who would trade places with us in a heartbeat. We need to notice the not-so-ordinary miracles happening every day.

If you want to see God bless you and manifest His presence in your life, start thanking God for the not-so-ordinary miracles. I will guarantee, in the long run, you will grow more and influence more people because of the challenges in your life than you ever could if you only experienced the blessings.

I've learned to thank God for the challenge we face—autism. Why? Because, without a doubt, I'm a better husband, father, and friend because of what we've been through. I've learned to not just love, but to love unconditionally. I see the miracles of life that other people may never see. I've had the opportunity to watch God use my son's life to overcome the challenges of autism and to affect people all over the world. In some ways autism was a gift to change and mold our family to bring hope to others.

What are some practical ways to recognize the little miracles every day? Let me share a few I've learned. Every morning when I pray, I thank God first for things I normally might take for granted. I thank God for food to eat. What a privilege it is to have food to eat when there are so many who are starving or malnourished. The United Nations Food and Agriculture Organization estimates that nearly 870 million people of the 7.1 billion people in the world—or one in eight—were suffering from chronic undernourishment in 2010–2012. Almost all the hungry people, 852 million, live in developing countries, representing 15 percent of the population of developing counties. There are 16 million people undernourished in developed countries.[3]

A friend of mine is a principal at a school in the Fifth Ward of Houston, and they are having to give free breakfast and lunch to students because, if they didn't, many children would not eat at all some days. You think it's happening in third-world countries, but it may be happening in your own backyard. So, every day, when you look in your refrigerator or cabinets and see even a small amount of food, you realize that what might seem ordinary to you is not ordinary to someone else. When you think about it, every day you have food is a day to celebrate another miracle God has given.

To remember the miracles all around me, I also thank God for a house to live in. As I walked through the slums of Calcutta, India, and saw the conditions of people living in makeshift tin houses with narrow alleyways and no space in between, I thought, *How can anyone live in conditions like this? How sad and miserable they must be.* Yet when I talked to many of them, they were not sad and miserable. For the most part they were happy and thankful they had a roof over their heads and a communal toilet in the ground to use. They didn't even mind taking sponge baths in the alley with their clothes on. Surprisingly, they looked happier than some people in America I know who have ten-bedroom houses.

I own a house in a middle-class neighborhood that is more than my family will ever need. I often walk through my house and say, "Thank You, God, for a house to live in. This is a gift from You, and please never let me take it for granted." If you look at what you have as a possession, and not as a gift, you will never see the miracle. We hold on to possessions, but we receive gifts. When you look at the house you live in as a gift, thankfulness will usually follow. If you look at your house as something you earned, entitlement will make you think you deserve it. It's tough for us to be thankful for what we have when we don't notice what we have. Homelessness, just like special needs, is invisible to most people—even to the ones closest to us.

How would you like to look back at your life and realize that, even in what seemed ordinary, God was doing not-so-ordinary miracles? We have so much to be thankful for, but to see it, we need to intentionally recognize all God is doing.

Try this exercise. Every day I thank God for the things I have in my life right now that seem normal, but without which my life would be totally different. So I made a list of at least ten things:

1. A personal relationship with God
2. My wife, kids, and family to love
3. Friends
4. Food to eat and water to drink
5. A house to live in
6. Clothes to wear
7. A job

8. A car to drive
9. A church to go to
10. A healthy body to live in

When I wonder where I would be without any of those things in my life, I realize that every day I'm blessed with them is a miracle from God. Where would I be if not for the grace of God? What would my life be like without my wife, kids, and family? How alone would I be if I didn't have friends? How hard would life be if I had no food to eat and water to drink? I would die. What would life be like if I were homeless and had no decent clothes to wear? What financial problems and relationship problems would I face if I didn't have a job? How hard would it be if I had to walk everywhere? What would my life be like if my religious freedoms were taken from me? How different would my life be if I were sick all the time?

When you put it in those terms, you realize how blessed many of us truly are and that every day is a miracle. You've heard the saying, "You don't know what you've got until it's gone." I have another saying: "You don't know what you've got because you forgot."

With Connor, we try to keep an eye out for everyday miracles. We even started a website called ConnorMoments. com to record all our special moments with him. The other day he wasn't feeling well and had to go to the doctor to get an X-ray of his stomach. When the machine moved over his stomach, Connor said, "Tummy, say 'cheese!'" Another time Connor dropped a puzzle piece in the car, and he said,

"Uh oh!" Samantha picked it up and gave it to him, and he responded, "There it is! Great job!" Then he clapped for her. One time we asked Connor who he loves. He said, "Mommy, daddy, sister, brother, and the pizza man." We cherish these moments because there was a time he didn't speak at all.

Let me encourage you to do a few things. First, thank God for the droughts, not just the breakthroughs. Second Corinthians 12:9 says, "My grace is all you need. My power works best in weakness. So now I am glad to boast about my weaknesses, so that the power of Christ can work through me."

Second, look around you every day and notice there are miracles happening everywhere. You don't have to be given a million dollars to experience a miracle. If you simply woke up today, that's a miracle, considering more than 151,600 people in the world died during the last twenty-four hours.[4] But you may say, "You don't know what I've been through." I would say to you that if it happened, God can use it. Find the miracle in it.

Finally, declare, "All is well," even when it's not. The Enemy can't fight back when you give him nothing to respond to. If you can find joy in the pain, you've taken all the power from the Enemy and given all authority back to God to perform a not-so-ordinary miracle in your life. Agree with God that you will listen for His voice and act accordingly. His plans for you are for good and not for evil. Thank God every day for the not-so-ordinary miracles.

ELEVEN

Stop Renting, Start Owning

When Connor was five years old, we were dealing with serious meltdowns with him. He would go into a frenzy when he didn't get his way, and we knew it wasn't just a child acting out. It seemed to be a stronghold in his life that we could not help him work through. One time Connor got so upset that he threw himself on the floor and started slapping his hands on the tiles. Then he got up and ran through the house screaming, with us chasing after him. It seemed like he was in pain but he didn't know how to tell us what hurt. I finally caught up with him in the bathroom, threw my arms around him, and we fell into the bathtub.

We were both crying at the same time. I think both of us felt helpless. I just kept whispering to him, "I love you, Connor. I love you, Connor." He would say, crying, "I love you, Daddy. I love you, Daddy." I remember sitting in that bathtub holding my son, tears streaming, and feeling so broken.

The next morning I heard God speak to me deep down in my spirit. He simply said, *If you want this situation to shift, stop renting My Word, and start owning My Word.* At that time my devotional life was consistent, but not as intimate as I wanted it to be. I had been allowing distractions to get in the way. The busyness of life crept in, and I had accepted that there were days when I could do more with God, and days when I settled for less.

Then God reminded me of a devotional I had read. It was based on Proverbs 4:20–21, which says, "My son, give attention to my words; incline your ear to my sayings. Do not let them depart from your eyes; keep them in the midst of your heart."

Right then I realized that if I wanted this situation to shift, I had to be willing to do the one thing: put God first. I couldn't store God's Word in the garage of my heart and take it out only when I needed it.

Then I remembered something I heard about an amazing woman of God, Dodie Osteen, who in the early 1980s was diagnosed with metastatic cancer of the liver and given just a few weeks to live. She looked up thirty scriptures that talked about healing. She was so sick, and her body was so frail, that she had turned yellow, but she put pictures up all over her room of herself when she was healthy, so she could get a vision of victory. Then she took those thirty healing scriptures from God's Word, and every morning when she got up, she spoke those scriptures over her life. Every day for weeks, she repeated this process. What was she doing? She wasn't renting God's Word; she was owning God's Word. The Bible says that the Word of God is alive and powerful, sharper than any two-edged sword (Heb. 4:12).

A few months later Dodie Osteen went to the doctor's office, and to the doctor's amazement, they could not find any cancer. A miracle of huge proportions had taken place. When you ask Dodie what happened, she will tell you that she believes it was the prayers of others and standing on God's Word that shifted her death sentence. I figured if God could do it for Dodie, why couldn't he do it in our situation?

We took the same healing scriptures Dodie had spoken over herself, and we spoke them over Connor every day. On the way to school we spoke them. Before he went to bed, we spoke these scriptures over him. We were tired of renting God's Word and hoping things would change. We were ready to own God's Word and declare it was changing. We didn't realize that not only was God listening, but Connor was listening. Every day he would get up and say, "Speak healing scriptures, Mommy and Daddy?" We also didn't realize that he wasn't just listening, he was memorizing them. He memorized all thirty healing scriptures. He started quoting them all through the day.

One day when Connor had cut his foot on something, I was holding him, and Sam was putting hydrogen peroxide on his foot. With a sad look on his face he said, "Is anyone among you sick? Let him call on the elders of the church, and they will pray over him." He was expressing his feelings through God's Word. That is amazing for an autistic child to do. Not only were Samantha and I owning God's Word, but Connor was owning it too. We knew that something was about to shift.

Then one day, after three years of dealing with melt-downs, it was as if God took His finger and pushed a red button that said STOP. And Connor's meltdowns stopped. It was a miracle. We could hardly believe it. But we *did* believe that when we started owning the Word of God, something powerful took place—something that we had tried so long to fix, God healed because we did the one thing that He requires. We put Him first.

God is not asking you to fix your life. He's so good to us that, even when we rent His Word, He will still bless us. Yet we will discover a whole other level of favor and provision when we start owning our relationship with God. You're His child. You don't get second best when you claim your birthright. We must start believing we are sons and daughters of the One who owns it all. You don't have to just get by; you can do great things. If you're willing to do the little extra, God will take your ordinary and make it extraordinary.

What are you going through today? I want to encourage you to do the little extra and find scriptures that speak about what you are dealing with. If you don't know where to find them, ask a friend or a pastor who does. If you have a financial need, find scriptures that talk about God's provision and blessing. If you're dealing with a difficult relationship, find scriptures that deal with relationships.

Whatever your need, find the scriptures that speak to that need. Then begin to speak those scriptures every day. Take your devotional life with God to another level, and watch God begin to work behind the scenes on your behalf. Supernatural doors require supernatural keys. These keys are not found in your hand. God places them in your heart. I wonder what great experience awaits beyond the next door. I'm convinced you will experience all the benefits of owning God's blessings. It's your time to stop renting and start owning the promises in the Word of God.

Too many of us have been taught an impoverished way of thinking when it comes to our spiritual inheritance. We forget there are God-given rights and benefits that come with being a child of God. When you receive an inheritance, provision is passed down like a legacy from generation to generation. You don't have to hope God will give it to you. It's your God-given inheritance. He is your heavenly Father, and you are His child, and with that endowment everything that He owns, you own. Everything that He has, He desires for you to have. It doesn't matter what you've done; when you accept Jesus as your personal Savior, it only matters that you carry His birthright as a child of God.

The last thing the Enemy wants you to remember is to whom you belong. He wants to keep your psyche pauperized. I'm not talking about being humble. Yet the Enemy will trick us into thinking that if we want all God has for us, that is greedy. You must understand that the Enemy will do anything to keep you mentally and spiritually bankrupt to settle for less, when God wants to do more.

When we believe things happen based on what we put our hands to rather than by God's provision, instead of allowing Him to fix our lives, we use God like duct tape. We use Him when we need Him. On the outside we might look good, but on the inside we are held together by casual Christianity. We are still going to heaven, and God still takes care of us, but we miss out on the rest of our inheritance. We will look back with too many regrets.

What's your greatest regret so far? Don't look back on your life and say, "I wish I had been happier." The first part of your life may have been difficult, but you need to get this deep down inside your spirit: the next part of your life can be different. Maybe in the past you've settled for the just-get-by-life, and you are deciding today that you don't want to look back one day and see unfinished dreams, wasted time, wishes that never came true, or things you wished you had done differently.

Make the shift from renting to owning not only God's promises, but your life. Own your mistakes, and see God turn your circumstances completely around. In your work, own it by being the best you can be, and watch God give you favor and promotion. In your school, own it, and watch good grades and scholarships come your way. In your relationships, own it, and watch your marriage go higher. If you are single, watch God give you the perfect mate or the best possible purpose for the single life you lead. Don't settle. Believe!

Too many times we get our performance mixed up with who we are. Just because you failed doesn't make you a failure. God knows it's impossible for people to be perfect and give Him everything, so God makes it simple and looks at the one thing. Matthew 6:31–33 says, "Don't worry about these things, saying, 'What will we eat? What will we drink? What will we wear?' These things dominate the thoughts of unbelievers, but your heavenly Father already knows all your needs. Seek the Kingdom of God above all else, and live righteously, and he will give you everything you need."

What is God asking of us? If we put God first place in our lives, He in turn will add all these blessings to us. Seems simple enough. Of course, what seems simple never is. Many times the Enemy is bent on keeping you from doing the one simple thing you need to do: put God first. The Enemy doesn't need to destroy you. He just needs to distract you.

We will never be able to eliminate all distractions, but we can be intentional and practice God's presence—to go from renting God's presence when we need it, to owning it. There is so much power available when we invite God into our daily routine. To put Him first, we need to welcome His presence daily—even hourly. Too many times we call on God only when we think we need Him, but the truth is that we need Him all the time. We are just too distracted to remember Him.

At one of our staff meetings, I put a picture of Jesus on a chair, with an agenda in front of it, and told everyone who came in for the meeting who tried to sit in the chair, "I'm sorry, but this seat is taken." They looked at me with a strange look on their faces, like, *What are you talking about? No one is sitting in the chair.*

I was trying to show them how powerful it would be if we put God first all through the day. If we owned His presence as if God were right there in the room with us. When we need wisdom, He's right there to answer. When we need direction, He's right there to show us which way to go. When we need a word from God, we can ask Him to speak to us. As believers, we may know God is everywhere, but often we forget to acknowledge He is even in the room. One of the most important lessons we can learn is to seek God's face (who He is) and not just His hand (what He can do for us).

When we ask God to be with us throughout our day, God already knows what He can do. What He wants is for us to acknowledge He can do it. He wants us to have the faith to go from renting to owning God's promises, presence, and Word in our lives.

One Sunday we were in the middle of the worship service at our church when I got a text from Norma Puga, our Champions Club director. I know I probably shouldn't have checked my phone during worship, but it kept buzzing in my pocket. It said, "You need to come to the Champions Club right away and see what Connor is doing."

My first thought was, *Is he having a meltdown?* It's funny—when you have a special-needs child and get an urgent message, your mind always goes to what's wrong instead of what could be right.

I walked out of the main sanctuary while the congregation was singing, and as I opened the door to the Champions Club room, there was Connor laying hands on the teachers' heads. From what I could tell, he was praying over them and speaking Scripture. Suddenly, I heard him say, "Scripture says that faith comes by hearing and hearing by the Word of God. Start to believe what God's Word says. Today let the flames of your faith be ignited by the Word of God. If you have faith as small as a mustard seed you can say to this mountain, be removed. God is moving mountains in your life that were once there."

I stood there watching and listening, stunned. I picked up my phone to video what was happening, because I had never seen a special-needs child do something quite like this. I knew God was in the room in a tangible and powerful way.

He continued praying scriptures over the teachers. I heard him say, "Today, be encouraged. You are simply going through a process. Your circumstances, if you will give them to God, will work for your good. Don't become bitter. But in it all know you are of priceless value. You are being transformed into an object of rare beauty. Beloved, I pray that you may prosper in every way just as your soul prospers." The adults had tears in their eyes as they received what this ten-year-old was speaking over them.

Then he began to speak scriptures of healing over their lives. He said, "Is anyone among you sick? Let them call for the elders of the church to pray over them and anoint them with oil in the name of the Lord." We did not know that one of the teachers had been battling cancer. She had just gotten a bad report after fighting the disease for five years. She said she felt as if he was praying just for her. For one hour he went from teacher to teacher in the Champions Club, laying hands on them and praying for them. It was extraordinary to watch.

Afterward the teachers said, "It was like he knew which scriptures to speak and that what he would say was exactly what we were dealing with." They were amazed. Connor had never done that at Champions Club before, and has never done it since. But God knew what those teachers needed, and He used a vessel open and willing to be used.

Never underestimate who God wants to use and what He can do. One time God asked me, *"Craig, how do you feel when you are underestimated?"*

I said, "I feel overlooked, undervalued, it's like they don't know my potential."

God said, *"I feel the same way when people underestimate Me."*

As you move from renting to owning, you'll realize the true value and potential of what you've been given as a child of God. Speaking the Word with authority, opening yourself up to God's presence, you'll find yourself becoming a vessel for God to pour through in the most extraordinary ways.

TWELVE

Creating a Grace Culture

A grace culture will never exist when we are unwilling to go the extra mile to extend grace without judgment. When someone is not like us, it is so hard to get past the differences and find the grace and love that needs to be conveyed to bring hope and healing. Today, because of the human condition, we continue to struggle with racial barriers, socioeconomic class wars, and stigmas based on our looks, abilities, and status. Often these stigmas have been passed down like a generational curse for the next person to inherit. Grace is the only way to combat it.

Recently I witnessed God's grace in an amazing way when my friend Karl Hagestrom asked me to speak about special-needs at a crusade in Africa. Thousands of people came from all over to hear about a God who loves them. I was very excited while we were waiting to go on stage to speak. As we were sitting in a hut near the venue, Karl leaned over and said, "You know, I'm not sure how these people are going to respond to your message tonight. You must understand there is a huge negative stigma concerning those with special needs."

One of the interns with us added, "Yes, even here at the crusade it's freaking us out a little bit. They are bringing kids who have special needs into the prayer tent and asking us to cast the demons out of these children, when we know they are just children with special needs. We are trying to explain to parents that their children don't have demons, they just have challenges."

This is a stigma in many third-world countries, but you can see frightening parallels in the way special-needs children used to be treated, and are sometimes treated even today in the West. In some tribes near where the crusade was held, special-needs children are hidden because they are considered a curse upon the family. The children may even be killed. A leader who works for Compassion International in Africa told me that some parents will take a rope and tie it around a brick and then tie the other end of the rope around the child's ankle and throw the child into a lake to drown. Some families may keep special-needs children outside at night to be eaten by wild animals. Those are extreme cases, but real ones.

In most cases, parents in this part of the world won't allow special-needs children to attend school or church or be seen in public because of the stigma. Kids in Africa with AIDS can go to school and church, but kids with special needs are not allowed. I met one little girl in Kenya who had autism and wanted to go to school so badly that she walked to school with her cousin. But she had to sit outside by herself while her cousin was inside learning. She had a smile that could brighten any room, but tragically, she was never allowed the same privileges other children were given. She got conditional treatment, based on her society's skewed view of her value. It was a society that had no room for grace for children like her.

As I waited to speak that day, after hearing all these things from Karl and the interns, I started to get a little nervous. There were no barriers between the stage and the people. If I said the wrong thing, I could be in trouble. I began to pray silently, *God, I know I am supposed to be here. I know You are using me and others like me to break down stigmas and allow Your grace to bring awareness and hope to special-needs families. Please show me You're with me as I speak today.*

Just then we heard a knock on the front door, and one of the attendants answered. It was a mother holding a child about six years old. The mother insisted on coming in, so Karl motioned her over and asked what we could do to help. As she sat down, she explained that her child had never walked and that he had been born crippled. He'd been ridiculed and excluded. She explained how difficult this was for her and her son, and she asked if we would pray that he would be healed.

I must be honest. In all my years in the ministry, I had never seen a child who had never walked stand up and walk. I had seen other miracles, but I had never seen this happen.

I thought Karl was going to pray for this child, since he was the big-time crusade speaker. But he smiled and turned to me and said, "I think you should pray for her son to be healed."

Nervously, I walked over to the mother and child. I felt

God's presence as I got closer. I asked the mother if she believed her son could be healed. She said yes, with tears rolling down her face. I told her to ask her son if he wanted God to heal him. She spoke to him, and he nodded his head. I told the interns who were standing next to me, "Here is what I want you to do. I don't want you to pick him up or help him in any way other than putting your fists out so he can put his hands on top of them for balance. If he wants to walk, then this will have to be God. God is going to have to do it."

As I began to pray, I cannot tell you exactly what I felt. It was as if a strong sense of the Spirit of God was all around this child. When I laid hands on the child, I could feel his legs were like rubber because of a lack of bone density. I felt bolder and bolder as the prayer went on. God's Spirit was present in that room. When I got through praying, I again told the interns to hold out their fists. I said to the boy, through the interpreter, "If you want to walk, grab their fists, and stand up and walk."

The little boy looked at his mom as if to ask, "Is this okay?" She nodded her head, and the boy reached out his hands, put his feet down to the ground, and shakily stood for the first time. He was wobbling back and forth, but standing. He took one step, two steps, and then, on the third, he fell. Even I was shocked. I couldn't believe what I was watching God do.

I got bolder and said, "The little boy is not finished walking. Reach down your hands and see if he wants to walk some more." The interns held out their fists, and the little boy pulled himself up from the ground and walked across the room and back to where he had been sitting. While this was happening,

I got so excited I pulled out my phone and took two photos of him walking. They show his mother looking on in amazement as her boy was being healed right before everyone's eyes.

The mother and boy walked out together, smiling and crying as God continued to do an astonishing miracle. When they left, I could hear God say in my spirit, *I just used you, through My power, to pray and bring healing to a child who couldn't walk. Is that confirmation enough that I am with you?*

That night I gave a message, saying, "Your children with special needs are not a curse; they are a blessing. God is going to use your special-needs children to do great things."

They didn't exactly roar approval at my message, but they didn't chase me off the stage either. You could tell they had never heard anyone say that a child with special needs was not a burden but a gift. Many lives were changed. Parents told us how they loved their children with special needs, and they asked how they could help them. Grace began to break through the stigma.

When I got back to the hut we had waited in before going on stage, I saw that little boy and his mother with huge smiles on their faces, ready to greet us. He stood right next to her. Grace had come into that community. Curses were replaced with declarations of blessing. Burdens were replaced with gifts. Where fear, violence, and rejection had reigned, healing came in, in more ways than one. God had chosen to bend down and heal this little forgotten one and to start a process of healing in the hearts of the people who had lived in a tradition of exclusion and cruelty. I believe they started looking at children with special needs a little differently that day.

When you look at the society we live in, how much real grace do you see, or how much of it is conditional? What would unconditional grace look like? God's grace. The truth is we can never fully understand the depth of God's grace. It's so far beyond what a human can comprehend that we can't convey grace without pointing to God, because outside of God we don't understand it. If we always gave other people the kind of grace that God has given us, we would see little or no crime, little or no racism, little or no divorce, little or no hate, little or no judgment. We would also see little or no fear and avoidance of the special-needs community, and more positivity, love, and nurturing.

Heaven is a place of complete grace. That's why the Bible says there will be no more crying or pain; by grace, all sin has been removed completely in heaven, and we are transformed through the resurrection. That same grace is activated here on earth through the cross of Jesus. When God answers you in your most undeserving moment, that is grace.

Yet we put limitations on what God gives unconditionally. We choose who gets more grace and who gets less. If you please enough people with your effort, you will get more grace. If you commit a certain type of sin, you might be qualified for more grace than if you committed another. I'm so glad God looks at it differently.

Grace is what you might call God's eraser. But it's so

much stronger than we can understand fully. And often it's completely foreign to human nature. We all want to be forgiving, but how hard is it to truly forgive? I would even venture to say that it would be impossible for any human being to forgive the way it's commanded in Matthew 18:21–22, unless that person were Jesus.

In Matthew 18, Jesus Himself showed Peter the perfect example of how marvelous grace is. Peter came to Jesus and asked him, "Lord, how often should I forgive someone who sins against me? Seven times?"

Jesus answered Peter, "No, not seven times, but seventy times seven."

I'm sure Peter thought to himself, *How could anyone forgive that many times? Are you serious, Jesus?* Peter thought he was being liberal by offering Jesus seven times more forgiveness. After all, seven is the number of completeness and plurality. But Jesus was showing him that, if you want to understand grace, forgiving someone *seventy* times is still not close to how much grace God has shown.

The New Covenant represents true grace that is not weighed or measured but freely given. We want grace to be logical, but I find true grace is usually not logical. But it doesn't have to be logical to be true. John 1:17 says, "The law was given through Moses, grace and truth came through Jesus Christ." Jesus brings grace and truth together.

So, as humans with an imperfect understanding of grace, how can we come even close to creating a grace culture in our lives, jobs, and families? Again, we will never master grace in our human condition. It is always available through God, but reciprocating it is a *choice* we make every day. The more you *give* grace, the more you will understand grace, and the more you can walk in grace. Sometimes it doesn't take 180-degree turns to start giving more grace. Usually, it just takes 90-degree tweaks in how you respond to people.

First, you can tweak your everyday interactions by viewing everything through the filter of love. We have a refrigerator that has a water filter in it. If the water is left unfiltered, we can still drink it, but it will have particles, and the water might leave a bad taste in our mouths. It's the same in the way we look at and talk to people. If we depend on our human condition, without a love filter, we will usually leave a bad taste in someone's mouth. *With* a love filter, we can give everyone we meet a taste of grace.

Take, for example, the area of conflict. Next time you deal with a tense situation or believe someone to be in the wrong, what if you used the filter of love—what if, instead of *challenging* them, you *encouraged* them? If you want someone to change, or you want someone to turn around, there is nothing wrong with challenging them. If you have a good, trusting relationship with that person, he or she will probably receive what you say. But if you don't have a close relationship, you may get a defensive response.

Activate the filter of love, and practice combining your

challenge with genuine encouragement. You will give them no reason to be defensive, and your grace-filled words can bring progress instead of division.

When you are trying to create a grace culture, love needs to be at the center of everything you are doing, otherwise grace will be hard to give. If it's not, we will try to speak the truth without love (being too harsh) or give grace without the truth.

We find more wisdom about this in 1 Corinthians 13, which says,

> If I could speak all the languages of earth and of angels, but didn't love others, I would only be a noisy gong or a clanging cymbal. If I had the gift of prophecy, and if I understood all of God's secret plans and possessed all knowledge, and if I had such faith that I could move mountains, but didn't love others, I would be nothing.

In other words, you can have all these gifts, but if you don't run them through the love filter, they are as good as counterfeit. There will be holes in our organizations. Hurt in our homes. Distrust in our society. A true grace environment cannot exist openly when there is manmade grace operating within its very culture. Grace must flow from the influencers down to every level until the majority is speaking the same language.

You can create a grace culture by not judging others. The Bible says in Proverbs 19:11, "Good sense makes one slow to anger, and it is his glory to overlook an offense." Again, we cannot erase failure from our mind like God can. He throws it into the sea of forgetfulness, and we throw it into the sea of "I'll forgive, but I can't forget." This doesn't make us bad people; but it is why Galatians 6:1–3 reminds us that we are human. Just because we're not in the wrong doesn't mean we won't fall when we allow pride to tell us that we are better than someone else because we didn't mess up like they did. This is where counterfeit, manmade grace is usually distributed. We tell others that our form of justice is the right course of action, and we have done the best we could do based on their failure. We say all the right things, but our thoughts and actions do not exhibit God-made grace.

If you want to create a grace culture in your home, church, or business, look at the temperature of grace in your life. Let it start with you. Practice grace. Every day, look for ways to show grace to someone. Include grace in your daily routine. Are you teaching grace through your example to your children? Are you letting go of offenses? Are you dealing with any unforgiveness in your life? Are you intentionally letting go of negative mind-sets that have been passed down from your friends and relatives? Are you letting go of pride and selfishness when you realize they're motivating you?

Search for scriptures and stories in the Bible in which grace was given when people failed. Be willing every day to go the extra mile to extend grace, even when someone may not deserve it. Test your thoughts so that your first resort is understanding and not judgment. Are you sarcastic and negative in your attitudes? There are always going to be negative people in your life who, no matter what you do, will not be on your side. Don't hang around negative people. As the saying goes, they always have a problem for every solution.

I'll admit, this is a daily process for me, too, and it will continue to be. But I encourage you to keep going in this process, like tending a garden. In our subconscious we may not know how much we devalue grace by our hidden discriminations and judgments, and even by our pride and selfishness. That's why we hold ourselves accountable to the grace of God. We must allow God daily to weed out what shouldn't be there and to grow what should be there.

If you ever felt the Holy Spirit nudge you to do something, you'll know it's important to respond. There is always something deeper happening when the Holy Spirit speaks. One Sunday I felt the Holy Spirit nudge me to not go into the main service but to go into the Champions Club. I didn't know why I felt it that day, but it was strong.

I left in the middle of the main service and went into the Sensory Room. As I walked in, I saw amazing volunteers working one-on-one with each special-needs child. There was such love in the room. One volunteer was working with a little boy with severe cerebral palsy to help him speak. She saw me and said to the boy, "Look, Matthew, there is Pastor Craig. Can you say hi to Pastor Craig?"

It took him a minute or two, but with everything in him, Matthew got those three words out: "Hi, Pastor Craig!" Then the volunteer said, "Oh, Matthew, you did that so well. You are amazing. I'm so proud of you, and so is God." A big smile came over Matthew's face.

I walked over to another child who was working on a sensory directional board where you can push certain buttons and the light changes direction. The teacher was telling a little girl with Down syndrome to push the right and left buttons. Every time she did, the teacher said, "You are so smart. I can't believe how much you've grown and developed. You know your numbers, letters, and now your directional signs. God is so proud of you." The little girl looked up at her and laughed after being affirmed. She went right back to the directional board to show the teacher she could do it again.

I walked over to the other side of the room, and there was a boy named KJ who had been fighting cancer for many months. KJ and his parents were seeking treatment at MD Anderson hospital, and if you've ever known a family battling cancer for long periods of time, and have watched their lives before cancer and after cancer, which usually involves moving from their home to a hospital. It's overwhelming, and it's usually that way for several years. It takes everything families have to fight for their children. When they can bring their children to Champions Club and then sit in a church service, it is like a cool cup of water in a hot desert.

We didn't know it at the time, but KJ was in his final days. But his parents, along with everyone at Champions

Club, were still believing for a miracle. We knew it was a bad situation, but no one was giving up. KJ was so sick he couldn't open his eyes, and as the worship music played softly and the calm lighting filled the room, I saw the teacher rubbing KJ's hand and hugging his bald head whispering these words: "KJ, I am so proud of you. You are such a fighter. You never give up. You inspire me to never give up no matter what I'm facing in life. What a champion you are." Tears were rolling down her cheeks and tears began to stream down mine.

I had never before felt such love in one room in my entire life. The presence of God was so strong you could almost reach out and touch it. I asked God, *"Heavenly Father, what am I feeling in this room? There is so much love and grace here."*

God spoke to me and said, *"Craig, this is the closest on earth to what heaven feels like. You see, Craig, these children with special needs don't fight the same battles you fight with pride and selfishness. No matter what you do, because you are typical, you will fight things that will try and block My grace and My glory. You will become consumed with trivial things like how you look, how someone treated you, what you did or didn't accomplish.*

"Many are so busy chasing success they forget about what's important. No matter what you do and how hard you work, because you are a typical human being, you will try to steal some of My glory. But with these kids, they don't deal with a lot of the same things you deal with. My glory is not blocked from shining down on them.

"It's like your son Connor. He has no idea I am using him to touch people all over the world. He doesn't deal with pride like that. His life is simpler. That's why I can use him to an even greater degree, because

he won't steal My glory. What you are feeling in this room is My glory shining down on these children and filling this room. This is what heaven feels like on earth."

I had to sit down. I had to take a minute to understand what God was teaching me. I realized these kids were not the *least* of these; they were the *best* of these. Not because they were better than anyone else, but they were greater vessels for God to use because they didn't fight the things that tend to hold others back. Our job is not to hide them but to bring them to the forefront so God's glory can be revealed through their lives.

If we will speak hope and love over people instead of judgment, we will see a culture of grace infiltrate our homes and communities. The filter we use to speak over people will determine what comes out on the other end. We may start looking at people's hearts and not their skin colors, backgrounds, or abilities. We will have hearts of inclusion and not exclusion. We will see real healing take place in the lives of those who have failed, and in the lives of those who face daunting challenges.

When selfishness ends, happiness begins. I believe with God's help we have the capacity to create a culture of grace in our lives that will bring value to every life we touch.

THIRTEEN

God Is Fighting for You

It was called the Thrilla in Manila—Muhammad Ali and Joe Frazier's third and final boxing match. Frazier had won the first bout, and Ali the second. The last fight would test both of their wills and stamina unlike any fight they had been in before.

The fight took place at 10:00 a.m. local time in the Philippines on October 1, 1975. Officials said the time it started was for international viewing audiences, but it was the worst time to hold a fight because of the humid and hot weather conditions. They were in an aluminum-roofed stadium, and that added to the heat. It was so suffocating you almost couldn't breathe.

They battled for fourteen rounds, taking shot after shot, in temperatures that some say reached 120 degrees. After the fourteenth round, and with Joe Frazier's eyes almost completely shut, his trainer Eddie Futch threw in the towel that ended the fight. People would call it the greatest fight in the history of boxing. Even though Ali won the fight, he felt the effects. During his fourteen fights that followed the Thrilla in Manila, Muhammad Ali wasn't the same.

After the Thrilla in Manila, Joe Frazier wasn't the same either. Ali had called him so many names leading up to the fight that Frazier felt he had suffered under a barrage of verbal abuse. Although it was just Ali's way of getting into the head of another fighter, Frazier would never forgive him for it. He chose to call Ali "the Gorilla." Until Frazier's dying day, it was reported he couldn't understand why Ali treated him that way, and he could never let the hatred completely go.

How many of us have felt like we just went fourteen rounds with our own enemy? It may not have been physical, but it was a mental and spiritual fight. As a matter of fact, it might as well have been physical for the toll it's taken on you and your family. You were pummeled repeatedly by depression, fear, anxiety, and pain. You may have come through the fight, but it was so difficult, you will never be the same.

I have seen divorce pull apart couples and families. Sometimes they have gone through so much, they don't even recognize themselves anymore. The punches of distrust, betrayal, and hateful words have gone back and forth for so long, they forgot that they had cared deeply about one another. We have felt the challenges of being special-needs parents when the punches of life so deflated us that we wondered if there would ever be relief. I've seen people who have lost their jobs (the first blow), and then they feel like they've lost their dignity (the second blow), and if they keep on taking punches, they wonder if the fight is worth it.

One of the Enemy's strategies is to pick a fight and get us in the ring. The struggle is real. The attacks are frequent. They range from physical (health related) to financial to verbal and relational assaults that are designed to not just stun you but also knock you out. Whatever the obstacle is in your life, the Enemy wants you to think and sleep on that problem until he has beaten you to a pulp. But he can't do anything unless he gets you in the ring.

Your response to the Enemy's taunts will determine whether you get in the ring. He can't hurt you if he can't reach you. You can't be scathed if you don't accept the challenge. We have been taught that when opposition comes against us, the best thing we can do is to defend ourselves. But our best defense is God's offense. God is fighting for us. He wants to fight for us. But sometimes we don't allow Him to do it. Every time we worry, we are putting ourselves in the ring with the Enemy. He's taunting us like a bully to get us in the ring.

When dealing with a bully, it's easy to feel powerless and all alone. The Bully Project describes bullying as complex and appearing in many different forms, but in general it is an action that is carried out deliberately to cause emotional or physical harm to another.[1]

As Christians, we are facing a similar bully called the Devil. He uses opposition in many forms to do his dirty work. Sometimes he uses thoughts in our minds to inflict the damage. The average person cannot defend himself or herself against the ridicule and shots the Enemy will shell out. They will try for a while, but the barrage of blame when someone has failed, or the hurt of a bad situation, gives the Enemy ammunition that he will use to defeat his opponent. That would be you or me. When you're facing a bully, you can't do it alone. If you don't tell someone, you may not make it through the battle. If you do make it through, you might be emotionally and physically injured.

You need an advocate who will fight for you. An advocate is a champion, upholder, supporter, backer, promoter, proponent, exponent, spokesman, campaigner, cheerleader, fighter, crusader, booster, and the ultimate flag-bearer. The advocate I'm talking about isn't just any advocate; He is the Creator of the universe. He is undefeated; He's never lost a fight in His life. Even when the Devil thought he had the Son defeated, He came back from what looked like defeat with the greatest return in the history of mankind. The Thrilla in Manila had nothing on this fight. It was the fight for the ages, and at the end, there was only one Champion.

There is no one stronger, no one greater, no one who wants to fight for you more than God Himself. Here is the key, though: if you worry or try to figure things out on your own, you are entering the ring with the Enemy. You are opening yourself up to a beat down. God never asked you to take the blows. He sent His Son to the cross to take the blows for you. Stop fighting the battles God means to fight.

In 2 Chronicles 20, three bullies were not only trying to

push the people of Israel around, they wanted to take them out. The armies of the Moabites, Ammonites, and Meunites came against King Jehoshaphat and his people. Let's just say it didn't look good. King Jehoshaphat knew they were in trouble. The Moabites and the surrounding nations marched against Jehoshaphat. That's what bullies do. They gang up on you. Have you ever felt ganged up on? It's tough defending things by yourself. The odds for the Israelites did not look good with three nations against one. But odds don't exist with God. The house of God always wins.

The enemy armies were set up and encamped at En Gedi. The king and his people were alarmed and afraid. They didn't stand a chance, and they knew it.

When you are surrounded by problems, are you going to let fear and despair overwhelm you, or are you going to let God defend you? This is a crucial time in a person's life.

Instead of giving up, Jehoshaphat cried out to God. He had a choice: He could stay afraid and start to worry and become distraught, or he could call out to God who was ready to fight for him.

When I was a kid, my dad thought I bullied my sister. I can't for the life of me see where he got that idea. Even though she was older, I always got in trouble. Of course, I was an angel. Well, maybe I could sometimes be in the wrong, but not all the time. You see, all my sister would have to do was yell, *"Daddy!"*

The next thing I would hear was my dad coming down the hallway of our house like the cavalry ready to defend my tattletale, back-stabbing sister. Before I knew it, I was toast. I'm still working through the emotional scars of my sister's wrongful, misguided accusations. (As you can tell, I still like picking on her . . . just a little bit.)

My sister followed Jehoshaphat's lead. When enemies surrounded them, he cried out to God, "O our God, will You not judge them? For we have no power to face this vast army that is attacking us. We do not know what to do; but our eyes are upon You." Translation: *"Daddy!"* Then, something powerful happened. In the silence, a man named Jahaziel, standing out in the crowd, shouted a bold declaration from God: "Listen, all you people of Judah and Jerusalem! Listen, King Jehoshaphat! This is what the Lord says: Do not be afraid! Don't be discouraged by this mighty army, for the battle is not yours, but God's."

Bam! There it is! The ultimate declaration of victory. King Jehoshaphat was probably thinking, *Wait a second. We don't even have to fight?* He probably said to his royal attendant, "Did I hear that right?"

So how are Jehoshaphat and the people going to beat these bullies if they don't fight back? Remember: God's ways are not our ways (Isa. 55:8). When Dr. Martin Luther King Jr. came up against racism and prejudice, God told him to not fight back with force but to fight back with peace. I'm sure some in the black community thought that was ludicrous. You can't make a difference with peaceful marches when the enemy is using brute force. But God knows the best way to beat a bully is not physically but spiritually. The peace of God ultimately pushed back the oppression of a people during the Civil Rights Movement because the battle was not theirs. The battle was God's.

Yet, that declaration, "The battle is not yours, but God's," was not the end of the story. Jahaziel first declared God's promise, but then he gave them God's plan. God will never give a promise without a plan. Jahaziel said, "Tomorrow, go down against them. But you will not even need to fight. Take your positions; then stand still and watch the Lord's victory." In other words, go to where you are supposed to fight, but don't get in the ring. The Heavyweight Champion of the World will fight for you. He's your partner, saying, *You just take your position, give Me praise because praise precedes the victory, and watch Me do it.*

So King Jehoshaphat and the army of Israel went down to where the bullies were hanging out. They gave God praise all the way there, took their positions, and then watched God do it. The three armies that had come against Israel started fighting among themselves. They ended up killing each other while King Jehoshaphat and his army looked down in amazement at what they saw. When it was finished, not only had the three bully armies killed each other, the Bible says that they left more plunder than the army of Israel could even carry. It took them three days to carry back all the treasure left behind.

They didn't even get in the ring. God wiped out their

enemies, and they kept all the spoils of war. That's the difference between us fighting the battle and letting God fight for us. The Bible says that when they went back to their homes after the battle, all the other nations heard about what God had done and would not touch them.

God didn't just help them win the battle and carry more plunder than they could contain, He also fought the battles that were yet to come. They knew for sure, if God was for Israel, who could be against them? No one. That's the power of God fighting for us.

When I reflected on this story, God revealed something powerful in my spirit. He said to me, *"You see, Craig, when you worry and get depressed and try to figure things out, you are entering the ring with the Enemy and fighting a battle I was meant to fight. Here's how gracious I am, Craig. I am so gracious I still let you win that battle, but here's the difference. You walked away with only one day of plunder. If you would have let Me fight the battle, you would have walked away with three. You walked away worn out, with battle scars and memories that I never intended for you to carry.*

"If you would have let Me fight the battle, you would have come out unscathed. If you will let Me fight for you, I won't just fight the battle you are currently in, I will fight the battles yet to come."

Who are the bullies in your life? When you are thinking the worst, God is planning the best. You can get in the ring and take your chances, or you can go to where you're supposed to fight, take your position, give God praise, and then watch Him do it. I don't know about you, but I would rather sit ringside watching the punches than be in the ring taking the punches. The best part is that, when God fights for you, the only one getting demolished is the Enemy. It's no contest. God has never lost a fight. All you have to do is let God do it and take home the prize. The Enemy has just entered a no-bully zone, because God is fighting for you!

FOURTEEN

Ready to Be Used

You may be in a time of evaluation. Your life may not have gone as you had planned, and you're not sure what to do. But just because you've had a few bad breaks or taken some unusual turns does not mean your life is over. It may just mean a new beginning. There are exciting days ahead, if you will keep believing and put God first.

When you fail, society often views you as someone who is broken or needs to be fixed. God views someone who is broken as someone ready to be used. Did you know that distressed furniture is one of the most popular and valuable types of furniture you can buy? They say it provides aged character. If you look at the wood of distressed furniture, you see flaws. But the flaws make it valuable.

I have a scar over my left eye on my forehead. It came from playing sports when I was in elementary school in Gridley, California. We used to play touch football at recess, and I went for a long bomb to the deepest part of the field. I went back, put my hands up, and caught the ball over my head for the touchdown. A few steps later my eyebrow caught the wire from a chain link fence. It tore the skin over the top of my left eye. It hurt at the time. Blood went everywhere, but that didn't stop me from playing a week later. Those stitches were only an interruption. I got back in the game.

Later that year I not only caught touchdown passes at recess, but I made the Pop Warner football team and scored touchdowns there as well. Today, when I look at that scar, I don't think about the wire cutting my forehead and how much it hurt; I think about how I not only caught the ball but held on for the touchdown. Every year that story gets more heroic . . . But basically, I don't let the scar remind me of my pain; I let my scar remind me of how I overcame.

You may have a lot of scars from life so far. Do you look at them and only see hurt and pain, or do you look at them and see how you've overcome and are still standing? Some people live proudly but suffer quietly because they are unwilling to let go of their pain. Every time they look at their scars, feelings of hurt and rejection fill their minds, and they never have victory over them. It's time to let your scars become stars. Let go of your pride. John Gray says, "Your brokenness will have a perfume that pride can never produce."[1] Stop focusing on your hurts from the past and watch what God will do.

My friend and a member of our staff, Nick Nilson, played high school football for the Hononegah Indians in Illinois. He wore the number two, and his life was all about football. In one game alone he rushed for 268 yards and five touchdowns. College coaches were checking him out, and scholarship offers were coming his way. He was the big man on campus. He had it all: girls, parties, popularity, and it seemed like his life was all planned out. He was on his way.

But in the fourth game of the season in his senior year, Nick took the handoff on a sweep around the corner. As he was tackled, he could hear the ligaments pop and tear in his knee and his dream of playing college football was over. It had seemed like everything was going his way.

I'm sure that when he felt his injury, he not only felt the pain of a torn-up knee but also the pain of a lost dream. Nick could have stared at his scars, gotten depressed, and given up. But a friend invited Nick to a youth camp, and Nick heard about a God who could turn his scars into stars. At that camp, he accepted Jesus into his heart and began a new life that would influence more people than he ever could have by playing college football.

God called Nick into ministry, and now he is affecting thousands of people as one of the pastors of Lakewood Church.

Some people might look at Nick's story and say that it was dumb luck. Some only see what might have been. But thousands of people hear him speak every week and many have come to know Christ through Nick's ministry. They look at his tale as a great success story because of the way he's touched their lives. Nick saw his own dad come forward after Nick had spoken in a service, and he prayed with his dad to receive Jesus into his heart. In Nick's football days, people saw him wearing number 2. In God's eyes, Nick went from number 2 to number 1. Now he's changing the world.

A man named Saul was on his way from Jerusalem to Damascus to arrest followers of Jesus (Acts 9:3–20). He wanted to take them back to Jerusalem as prisoners, question them, and possibly execute them. The journey was interrupted when Saul saw a blinding light, fell to the ground, and communicated directly with a divine voice.

"Saul! Saul! Why are you persecuting me?"

"Who are you, Lord?" Saul asked.

And the voice replied, "I am Jesus, the one you are persecuting! Now get up and go into the city, and you will be told what you must do."

The men with Saul stood speechless, for they heard the sound of someone's voice but saw no one! Saul picked himself up off the ground, but when he opened his eyes he was blind. So his companions led him by the hand to Damascus. He remained there blind for three days and did not eat or drink.

Saul came in one way and was about to leave a changed man. The road you came in on may be different from the road you go out on. You can't plan what God has destined. This was Saul's divine interruption. He came to a place of brokenness, so God could use him. If you can't humble yourself before God, you will struggle when humbling yourself before man. When you lay things down, God will use you.

Saul was about to find out that the same persuasive gifts he had used to do wrong, God was going to use to do right. He was changing from Saul to Paul. The gifts he once used to sin, God would use to help others to win. Here's what the Bible says happened next:

> So Ananias went and found Saul. He laid his hands on him and said, "Brother Saul, the Lord Jesus, who appeared to you on the road, has sent me so that you might regain your sight and be filled with the Holy Spirit." Instantly something like scales fell from Saul's eyes, and he regained his sight. Then he got up and was baptized. Afterward he ate some food and regained his strength. Saul stayed with the believers in Damascus for a few days. And immediately he began preaching about Jesus in the synagogues, saying, "He is indeed the Son of God!"

Paul would become one of the greatest heroes of the faith. He is considered one of the most important figures of the apostolic age. Fourteen of the twenty-seven books in the New Testament of the Bible are attributed to Paul. He traveled from a road of destruction to a road of victory.

When you die to yourself, God is looking at a person He can use. The plans you had for your life just got bigger. He loves the underdog, the comeback story, the against-all-odds "You made it!" headline. That's where God shines. God desires restoration even more than we do. He will not rest until He's settled things.

We know a Champions Club is working when we see a Champion and their family moving from injured party to conquering warrior. When they are still going through extreme difficulty but, even in that unbelievable challenge, they find a way to rise above and testify to the goodness of God. Believe me: when the odds are stacked against you like they are for a special-needs parent, that's not an easy thing to do. I met a woman in Lanús, Argentina, who did just that. I was coming to speak at Presencia De Dios church in their services that weekend and then planning to go to one of their sister churches where a new Champions Club had been launched. I love the Argentinian people. They are so passionate. I've never been kissed so much in my life.

When I arrived to speak in the services I couldn't believe the crowds. They were lined up outside. I knew they weren't coming to see me, because I wasn't a well-known speaker; but Jonatan, my host, said they were coming to hear me because I represented them.

I said, "What do you mean? I'm nobody."

He said, "Not to them. They drove from all over because they feel you are one of them." It's true. If you have a special-needs child and you meet someone else who has been on the same journey, you have an instant connection. Even though your individual journeys may be different, you face very similar things.

I thought I was just coming to help dedicate a Champions

Club and preach, but I couldn't comprehend that I was representing a nation of special-needs people who had never been fought for by anyone from a place of influence. Now I was actually preaching about their lives from the platform. They were so responsive. I wanted to connect to the crowd by telling them I became of fan of soccer by watching one of their native sons, Lionel Messi, play. Lionel Messi is considered one of the greatest soccer players in history—if not the greatest. When I said that, you would have thought we were at a soccer game. They went crazy. Between services some of them even went home and brought back Argentina Messi jerseys—and the church's leader, Pastor Bernardo, and his team actually give me a signed Barcleona Messi jersey. I have it hanging in my office to this day.

When I finished speaking I tried to get back to the green-room area, but I couldn't get through the crowd. Families and organizations of people serving special-needs kids, teens, and adults were bringing their children up to me to give me a hug and kiss and ask me to pray for them or bless them. Some said they'd traveled hundreds of miles to get there. I asked them why they traveled so far, and they said, "You're the first one who's ever spoken for us." I looked at them in disbelief. I began to cry because I was beginning to see the magnitude of what this ministry meant to these families. Busloads of special-needs individuals were coming from far distances to hear someone say to them that they were going to do great things and that God has a destiny for their lives. For eight services, I got the privilege of connecting with and meeting these beautiful families. It was one of the greatest, most effective days of ministry I've ever experienced.

That evening we went to Iglesia Conexión Con Dios Church in Buenos Aires, which had launched a Champions Club for special-needs children in 2015. We were so excited to see all God had done since then. In just a few months, the Champions Club had close to eighty families attending. They had excellent leadership and an incredible team of more than thirty volunteers serving there.

After I spoke in the last service that day, they asked if I would come back to one of the classrooms and encourage and greet the many families and kids who attended Champions Club. I knew most of these families were rejected in their culture and hidden, with no real hope or future. Many families are taught to hide their children because they are an embarrassment or a curse as a consequence of sin in their life. Nothing could be further from the truth; but I was still expecting our meeting to be more focused on their many needs and struggles.

I told Jonatan to let the families know I would say a word of encouragement first, and if they have any needs we would be honored to pray for them. I then added, almost as an afterthought, "And, if any of them has a testimony of something that has happened since they started attending the Champions Club, we would love to hear it." But honestly, I didn't expect to hear many stories of victory in the face of all they were suffering.

We opened up the door and stepped in to a packed room

of special-needs parents and their children. Let me say—it was loud. They had been waiting for twenty minutes, and the kids were obviously getting restless.

I then began to encourage the parents and tell them what a gift their children were to this world and what heroes these parents were to us. When I asked for their needs, to my surprise, one parent after another began to share testimony after testimony of how God was using this ministry to help their children grow and develop.

I couldn't believe what I was hearing from these parents who were in such desperate circumstances. We went around the whole room, and not one parent presented a need, but every parent had a testimony of what God had done.

When that happens you know you have a successful Champions Club ministry. The first parent was a single mom with a severely autistic child. She lived north of Buenos Aires, but every Sunday got up at three in the morning to take her autistic son on a community bus for six hours just to get to Champions Club. They had to stop at every bus stop through every village to get there.

She said, "Iglesia Conexión Con Dios Church and Champions Club have changed our lives. My son, who was struggling in school, is doing much better now. His behavior is better, his comprehension is better, and he loves coming to the Champions Club—and I love being able to sit in an entire service and know that for the first time my child is being loved, accepted, and developed just like every other child."

All I could do was cry.

She could finally smile as she looked proudly down at her child with hope, and with victory.

We recently did a survey of fifty families from five Champions Club locations around the world, and the results show us what restoration and victory look like in progress:

- 86 percent of parents said that Champions Club has positively affected their child academically.
- 96 percent of parents have seen positive changes in their child's behavior since attending Champions Club.
- 93 percent of parents said that Champions Club has positively affected their child's social emotional growth (identifying emotions in self and others, sharing, empathy, making and maintaining friendships, asking for help, helping others, increased eye contact during conversations).
- 89 percent of parents said Champions Club has helped develop their child's gifts and talents in a positive way.
- 100 percent of parents said that Champions Club has positively affected their child's spiritual life.
- 96 percent of parents said that the four components of Champions Club (sensory, motor, education, and spirit) have benefited their child holistically.
- 100 percent of parents said Champions Club has benefited them as a family, allowing them to share in life experiences and attend church.

- 100 percent of parents said the services Champions Club provides (for example, church services and respite nights) have helped their marriage or family dynamics.
- 100 percent of parents said Champions Club has positively affected their home life.
- 75 percent of parents said Champions Club has helped their children transition into an inclusive environment.

We are beginning to see fruit that we never could have imagined when we started. When you take that step to build others, God will take it to places you could never dream of, and He will raise up new overcomers.

One thing overcomers have in common is that although they may have struggled with their faith, they never lost it. They found a core belief deep inside that said, "No matter how many times I fail, I will keep getting up and I will hold on to my dream."

If your life hasn't gone as planned, let me ask you a question: If you can't do anything else, can you still believe? It doesn't have to be a bold, confident declaration; it may be a quiet word under your breath saying, "I believe." Pastor Joel Osteen says, "Don't use your energy to worry; use your energy to believe."[2]

No matter how hard, worn-out, or dirty your past is, your future is spotless. Every disappointment, every wrong, every closed door has prepared you for your future. Failure may have paved the road to your greatest success.

The first part of my life was a journey in understanding my identity and my purpose on this earth. As I look back, I missed what was important more often than I recognized it. I had compassion for people but nothing like what was going to take place later. It doesn't make me better than anyone else, but it has made me become a better person. If you can see—truly see—people beyond their exterior and abilities, you become a part of them. You will share their hearts, and you will see them for who they are and who God created them to be.

God has shown me through Connor that even when Connor didn't know how to express his feelings, we could still feel his love. We see you, Connor. Even when you can't express how you feel, we see you. When you don't know how to deal with all your emotions, we see you. When you can't do things typical kids can do, we see you. We see what you can do that others can't. You have a purpose. Autism is your interruption, but you will touch people like no one else can. Along with your brother and sister, you are your mother's and my greatest accomplishment. You are a masterpiece. You are a gift. You are our cause.

On World Autism Day I don't celebrate autism. I celebrate the brave kids and families who fight it and overcome every day. Autism is not my cause. Special needs are not my cause. Connor is my cause. People are my cause. Passion is more powerful when there is a name and face attached to it.

I celebrate Connor and every child, teen, and adult who fulfills their purpose in spite of their challenges. I see them now! I will never look at them the same way again. My senses are alive for the hurting, broken, and forgotten. My unexpected challenge awakened me. It enlarged my heart. It broke my spirit so I could let love be poured out. It was the greatest gift God could bestow on me. Whatever you are going through, God is breaking you for something much bigger than yourself. It's your time to shine.

Connor is doing amazing today. He loves to sing, swim, and listen to music. He's an excellent student and is at the top of his class. He is drawn to spiritual things, and he can quote more than fifty scriptures. I can see him one day running the Champions Club and speaking to thousands.

I have watched God speak through Connor in such profound ways. A few years ago when we were eating dinner, I asked Connor what he wanted to be when he grew up. I was expecting the typical answer of a singer, a fireman, or a ball player. But without hesitation he looked at me and said, "I want to be grateful." I sat there stunned because I had never heard an eleven-year-old say that before. I knew God must have said it through him. I can't wait to see how God is going to use Connor in the future.

Acknowledgments

I am so grateful to my wife and children for all their support and inspiration. This book would not have been possible without them. We have walked on this journey from the very beginning together, and it has made us stronger and closer than ever. You are my human sunshine and my greatest accomplishment. I love you all so very much!

Thank-you to my mom Carol and my sister, Radonda, my brother-in-law Chris, and nephew and niece Justin and Julie. I am so blessed to have a family that laughs together, believes in each other, and loves each other as much as we do. Not many families can say that, but I thank God that we can. I miss you, Dad.

To all our friends and family: I call myself rich, not because I have money, but because I have you. I'm so grateful for all of you.

To my great friend, Clayton: I have never met a more loyal friend with such a servant heart as yours. You are more than a friend—you are a brother. Thanks for always cheering me on. Love you, Clayton!

Debra Jackson, you have been my armor bearer. We have worked together since the beginning at Lakewood, and I couldn't have a better partner in ministry than you, my dear friend. For every victory, you played a huge part in it. For every life influenced, you had a hand in it. You are a big deal. I love you, Miss Debra!

It's been my honor to serve with Joel and Victoria Osteen. There has never been a time when I've asked you to help those with special needs that you have not responded. Champions Clubs became a reality because you believed in helping those who needed it most. You have done so much for Connor and our family that it would take me a lifetime to express all our gratitude and thanks. We love you more than you will ever know.

I want to thank Dr. Paul and Jennifer Osteen for your amazing support and love. You've taught me what it means to be a true servant, and I will forever be grateful for your lives. Thank you also to Miss Dodie Osteen and all the Osteen family. Your support and love for our family has been immeasurable.

To the Lakewood staff: I cannot tell you what a privilege it has been for me to serve with you. I'm so glad to be a part of this family. I will never forget my time at Lakewood because of you.

A big thank-you to Norma Puga and the Champions Club team for special needs at Lakewood. What you do for children and families every week to bring hope to the brokenhearted is unbelievable. Your crown in heaven will be heavy from all your rewards. I love and appreciate you all!

To all the Champions Clubs across the world who are helping those with special needs: You are making a transformational difference in the lives of these families. It's going to be hard at times, but don't give up. They need what you have to give, and that is hope, healing, and love. You are making a huge difference in the lives of so many. Thanks for going on this journey with us.

Last, thank You, God, for all You've done for my family on this journey. You have taught us so much. I thought autism was a burden, and You showed me it was a gift. You showed us what it means to unconditionally love someone the way You love us. You showed us that our son has a great purpose and that he will ultimately be known for his abilities, not his disabilities. You showed us how we shouldn't waste our pain, and that the greatest thing we can do when we are hurting is to help others. But most of all, You showed us Your faithfulness. Through *everything* You remain *faithful*.

Notes

Chapter 2: Bend, but Don't Break

1. Disabled World, "Some Quick Disability Facts," https://
www.disabled-world.com/, accessed September 20, 2017.

Chapter 4: Baal-Perazim: The God of the Breakthrough

1. Sermon by Joel Osteen.
2. Emily Colson, *Dancing with Max* (Grand Rapids: Zondervan,
2012), 194.

Chapter 5: God Is Near to the Brokenhearted

1. Shannon Dingle, "Don't tell me your church's theology is
sound if my family isn't welcome," Church4EveryChild
(blog), March 18, 2015, https://church4everychild.
org/2015/03/18/dont-tell-me-your-churchs-theology-is-sound
-if-my-family-isnt-welcome-shannon-dingle/.

Chapter 6: Standing on the Shoulders of Giants

1. Sir Isaac Newton, letter to Robert Hooke dated February
5, 1675, from the Simon Gratz collection of the Historical
Society of Pennsylvania, accessed September 26, 2017,

http://digitallibrary.hsp.org/index.php/Detail/Object/Show
/object_id/9285.

Chapter 9: Out of the Drought

1. Eli Langer, "Chocolate Bar Resume Takes Internet By Storm," CNBC, February 21, 2013, https://www.cnbc.com/id /100482311?view=story&$DEVICE$=native-android-tablet.
2. Max Lucado, "Meet the God of Encouragement," MaxLucado .com, March 22, 2012, https://maxlucado.com/meet-the-god-of -encouragement/.
3. Mark Batterson, *The Circle Maker* (Grand Rapids: Zondervan, 2011), 9.
4. Ibid., 9–10.
5. Ibid., 10–11.

Chapter 10: Not-So-Ordinary Miracles

1. www.snappin.org.
2. Ibid.
3. Food and Agriculture Organization of the United Nations, "Globally almost 870 million chronically undernourished— new hunger report," October 9, 2012, http://www.fao.org /news/story/en/item/161819/icode/.
4. Population Reference Bureau and The World Factbook, Central Intelligence Agency.

Chapter 13: God Is Fighting for You

1. The Bully Project, "What Is Bullying?" accessed September 29, 2017, http://www.thebullyproject.com /tools_and_resources.

Chapter 14: Ready to Be Used

1. From a message at Lakewood Church.
2. @Joel Osteen, Twitter, September 3, 2013, https://twitter.com /joelosteen/status/374854526450565120?lang=en.

About the Author

Pastor Craig Johnson is currently the Director of Ministries at Lakewood Church in Houston, Texas. He oversees all pastoral ministries and staff and travels throughout the year speaking to organizations about the reality of special-needs families and the hope God has for them. In 2009, Craig launched the Champions Club, a state of the art facility for special-needs kids that features a physical therapy room, spiritual therapy room, sensory room, and an educational room. He is the co-creator of Champions Curriculum for special-needs families and is the author of the book *Lead Vertically*. As an enthusiastic advocate for special-needs children, Craig firmly believes the best is yet to come. Craig is married to Samantha and they have three children: Cory, Courtney, and Connor.

To find our more information
about how to launch a

CHAMPIONS CLUB

go to www.championsclub.org